SPECTRUM®

Test Prep

Grade 5

Published by Spectrum®
An imprint of Carson-Dellosa Publishing LLC
Greensboro, North Carolina

Spectrum®
An imprint of Carson-Dellosa Publishing LLC
P.O. Box 35665
Greensboro, NC 27425 USA

Printed in the USA • All rights reserved.   ISBN 978-1-4838-1378-3

03-025177811

Table of Contents

What's Inside?

Spectrum Test Prep is designed to help you and your fifth grader prepare and plan for success on standardized tests.

Strategies

This workbook is structured around strategies. A strategy is a careful plan or method for achieving a particular goal, such as succeeding on a test. Strategies can be broad, general ways to approach a test as a whole or a category of skills. Strategies can also be specific, providing step-by-step instructions on how to tackle a problem or offering guidelines on how to answer a question about a story. Learning how to apply a strategy gives test-takers a plan for how to approach a test as a whole and how to answer questions.

This workbook offers a set of broader strategies as well as very specific strategies. General test-taking strategies apply to all tests, and should be used to help prepare for the test. Specific strategies for English Language Arts and Mathematics tests are divided into larger categories of skills students will encounter, such as reading literature or performing calculations. On each practice page, you will find even more specific strategies that apply to the skills.

Test Tips

Test Tips are included throughout the practice pages. While strategies offer a plan for answering test items, Test Tips offer ideas for how to apply each strategy or how to approach a type of question. There are general Test Tips that apply to all tests as well as specific Test Tips for English Language Arts and Mathematics tests.

Practice Pages

The workbook is divided into two sections, English Language Arts and Mathematics. Each section has practice activities that have questions similar to those that will appear on standardized tests. Also included are strategies and Test Tips to guide students. Students should use a pencil to complete these activities.

Strategy Review Pages

Strategy review pages give your student an opportunity to review and practice important strategies in each content area. These strategies cover the important skills students will encounter on tests in English Language Arts and Mathematics.

Answer Key

Answers for all of the practice pages and strategy review pages are found in an answer key at the end of the book.

Test-Taking Strategies

Being prepared is key to doing your best on test day. Read the tips below to help you prepare for tests.

In the days before the test...

- Keep up on your reading, worksheets, and assignments. Completing all of your assigned work will help you be better prepared for the test.

- Don't wait until right before the test to review materials. Create a study schedule for the best result. That way, you can study a bit at a time and not all at once.

- Take advantage of sample items and practice tests. Complete these to practice for your test. If you run into concepts or skills that are new, ask a teacher or other adult.

The night before the test...

- Don't try to study everything all over again the night before. If you've been studying in the days before the test, all you need the night before is a light review of your notes. Remind yourself of the key ideas and practice a few skills, but don't study late into the night.

- Make sure you have all the materials you will need for the test, such as pencils, paper, and a calculator. Check with your teacher to make sure you know what tools to bring. Having everything ready the night before will make the morning less stressful.

- Get a good night's sleep the night before the test. If you are well rested, you will be more alert and able to do your best.

On the day of the test...

- Don't skip breakfast. If you are hungry, you won't be thinking about the test. You'll be thinking about lunch.

- Make sure you have at least two sharpened pencils with you and any other tools needed.

- Read all directions carefully. Make sure you understand how you are supposed to answer each question.

- For multiple choice questions, read all the possible answers before choosing one. If you know that some answers are wrong, cross them off. Even if you have to guess, this will eliminate some wrong answers.

- Once you choose or write an answer, double check it by reading the question again. Confirm that your answer is correct.

- Answer every part of a question. If a question asks you to show your work or to explain how you arrived at an answer, make sure you include that information.

- If you are stuck on a question, or are unsure, mark it lightly with a pencil and move on. If you have time, you can come back. This is especially true on a timed test.

- Breathe! Remind yourself that you've prepared for the test and that you will do your best!

Strategies for English Language Arts Tests

Read the strategies below to learn more about how they work.

Use details from the text to make inferences, understand theme, and draw out meaning.
Writers carefully choose details to include in their writing. Every detail matters. Each one is included for a purpose. As you read stories, look for details that help you understand what the writer is saying about characters, events, and the overall meaning, or theme. As you read passages, look for details that give reasons that support any opinions or facts the writer shares, as well as the central or main idea.

Identify literary or structural elements and use them to understand the meaning of a text.
Writers use literary elements such as figurative language to bring more meaning to their writing. They choose a structure that reflects their purpose for writing. Read carefully for ways that these elements help you understand the meaning of a story, poem, or passage.

Look carefully at visuals such as illustrations, diagrams, or graphs to see how they connect to the text.
Visuals are always related to the text. It is up to readers to figure out the connection. Does the visual explain something that is difficult to say in words? Does it add detail? As you read stories and passages, look carefully at visuals to see what information they provide.

Reread texts to make comparisons, draw conclusions, or support inferences.
Every reader has his or her own ideas about a text. If you are asked to draw a conclusion about what the writer means or thinks, however, you need to rely on details in the text, not your own opinions. When you have drawn a conclusion or made an inference, reread the text to make sure you can support it with facts, examples, and other information from the text.

Use word clues in a text to identify its structure, to see how ideas in a text are related, and to clarify word meanings.
Some words are signals that a text has a particular structure. For example, the words *so* and *because* often signal a cause-and-effect structure. You may also be able to use words as clues to the meaning of unfamiliar words.

When writing, use details to support, explain, or clarify your main ideas.
In persuasive and informational writing, it is important to make sure you support and explain each main idea with details. Facts, examples, and logical reasoning can all be used to make your main ideas strong and clear.

Use an outline to plan your writing.
Prewriting activities such as outlining can make writing clear and make your ideas easy to understand. A simple outline that lists main ideas or claims followed by their supporting details is enough to make your writing flow more easily.

Use transitions to show how ideas are related.
As you write, use transitions to help your reader follow your train of thought. You may know how your ideas are related, but readers need a little extra help! For example, the transition *As a result* shows that you are explaining a cause and an effect. The transitions *Next* and *Finally* help readers see that you are explaining a process or events that happen in a certain order.

Revise to make sure your writing is clear and makes sense. Then, edit to fix errors.
After you finish your draft, you may have time to revise and edit. First, revise to make sure your words say what you wanted them to say. Then, check spelling, capitalization, punctuation, and grammar to catch and fix errors.

English Language Arts

Quote Text to Support Inferences
Reading: Literature

DIRECTIONS: Read the story. Then, answer the questions.

Waterland

[1] "Hurray!" cried Meghan. [2] "Today's the day we're going to Waterland!" [3] It was a steamy July day, and Meghan's mom had agreed to drive her and her new friend Jake to the water park. [4] Just then, Meghan's mom emerged from her bedroom. [5] She looked exhausted and unhappy.

[6] "What's the matter, Mom? [7] Are you afraid to get wet?" Meghan teased. [8] Mrs. Millett sighed as she informed the kids that she was feeling unwell and far too tired to drive to the water park safely. [9] Meghan and Jake were disappointed. [10] "My mom has chronic fatigue syndrome," Meghan explained. [11] "Her illness often makes her really tired, but she's still a great mom."

[12] "Thank you, dear," said Mrs. Millett. [13] "Maybe I can't drive safely, but I can still create good ideas. [14] I bet you and Jake can construct your own Waterland while I rest in the lawn chair."

[15] Meghan and Jake quickly set up three different sprinklers. [16] One tossed a graceful arc of water high into the air, where the summer sun tinted it with rainbow hues; the others sprayed jerky bursts of water that swept across the lawn. [17] Then, the kids dragged the play slide over to the wading pool and aimed one sprinkler at the slide. [18] In no time, Meghan and Jake were soaking wet, and the humid July air lost its punch.

[19] "Thank you for being so understanding," Meghan's mom said later that afternoon. [20] "I feel better now, but I'm really hot! [21] There's only one cure for that." [22] She stood under the sprinkler wearing all of her clothes and laughing, until she was drenched from head to foot. [23] Meghan and Jake laughed too. [24] "Now you have chronic wet syndrome, Mom!" Meghan exclaimed, as mother and daughter shared a sopping wet hug.

Strategy — Combine what you already know about a topic and what a story says about that topic to make an inference.

Test Tip — When you quote a story to support an inference, make sure to include the exact words from the story and to place them inside quotation marks.

1. **A reader has made this inference: Getting wet helps people cool off in the summer heat. Which sentence correctly quotes the story to support this inference?**

   (A) After Meghan and Jake played in the water, the "hot July air lost its punch."

   (B) After Meghan and Jake played in the water, the humid July air lost its punch.

   (C) After Meghan and Jake played in the water, "the humid July air lost its punch."

   (D) After Meghan and Jake played "in the water," "the humid July air lost its punch."

2. **Which sentence contains words that a reader could quote to support the inference that Meghan loves her mother?**

   (A) Sentence 2

   (B) Sentence 11

   (C) Sentence 14

   (D) Sentence 18

Quote Text to Support Inferences
Reading: Literature

Strategy As you read, look for context clues in the same sentence as the word or phrase you want to understand. Also, look in the paragraphs that come before and after the word.

Test Tip After you make an inference, return to the story to review the details that support the inference. You may decide to add or change the details you use to support your inference.

3. **Which quoted words from the story best support the inference that Meghan and her mom have a playful relationship?**

   (A) " 'Today's the day we're going to Waterland!' " (Sentence 2)

   (B) " 'Are you afraid to get wet?' Meghan teased." (Sentence 7)

   (C) " 'Thank you, dear,' said Mrs. Millett." (Sentence 12)

   (D) " 'I feel better now, but I'm really hot!' " (Sentence 20)

   Write how you know.

   _____

   _____

   _____

4. **Which context clues help readers to understand that the word "chronic" in Sentence 10 describes an ongoing problem that cannot be quickly solved? Choose two.**

   (A) Meghan's mother's tiredness lasts all day.

   (B) Meghan says her mother is often very tired.

   (C) Meghan's mother says she cannot drive safely.

   (D) Meghan's mom thanks the kids for giving her time to rest.

   (E) Jake and Meghan take her mom's advice to make a water park.

5. **Write a few sentences that make an inference about Meghan's mom. Include quoted words from the story to support your inference. Be sure to quote the words exactly and to place them inside quotation marks.**

   _____

   _____

   _____

   _____

   _____

   _____

   _____

   _____

   _____

Name _____ Date _____

Determine Theme and Summarize Text
Reading: Literature

DIRECTIONS: Read the story. Then, answer the questions.

Pot o' Gold

[1] "Come on, Luisa," Marla begged. [2] "We agreed to help, and besides, we'll have fun." [3] Luisa frowned. [4] They had agreed to volunteer at their city's equine therapy center, and she didn't want to let the center down. [5] But, she hadn't reckoned with her fear of horses when she signed up. [6] Powerful, muscular horses intimidated her. [7] Luisa closed her eyes and imagined huge, hard hooves. [8] She could almost feel one stepping on her foot while she reluctantly pulled her boots on.

[9] Despite her fears, Luisa and her whole family believed strongly in giving back to the community, and the equine therapy center did such important work. [10] People healing after accidents, kids dealing with limited mobility, and even veterans coping with the stress of military service benefited from grooming and riding the specially trained horses. [11] Luisa wanted to be part of this work, but those horses—so huge!

[12] After the girls' parents dropped them at the center, a trainer called to Luisa. [13] "So glad you're here!" he said. [14] "Your first task is to muck out a stall and then carry in fresh feed." [15] He led the way to a stall door, and Luisa felt her chest tighten when she pulled it open. [16] There, to her shock, stood a horse not much taller than her family's dog. [17] "This is Pot o' Gold," the trainer said, "but we usually call her Goldie. [18] She's so gentle, even little children feel comfortable grooming her as part of their therapy." [19] He added with a smile, "And I heard you were a little horse-shy." [20] Gratitude and wonder rushed over Luisa. [21] "This pint-sized pony," she thought, "is *already* helping me!"

> ## Strategy
> Use ideas, events, and details from a story to determine its theme. As you read, find a story's theme by asking not what the story is about (its topic), but what a major character learns during the story about that topic.

1. Which problem in the story contributes most to readers' understanding of the theme?

Ⓐ The strength and size of horses frighten Luisa.

Ⓑ Injured people need therapists to help them heal.

Ⓒ The equine therapy centers needs volunteers.

Ⓓ Luisa's family insists that each family member give back to the community.

Write how you know.

_____

_____

_____

2. Which sentence best states the theme of "Pot o' Gold"?

Ⓐ When family members argue, they must try to forgive each other.

Ⓑ When people are injured, trained horses can help them heal.

Ⓒ When volunteers help, a community becomes a better place to live.

Ⓓ When people work together, they can face and overcome challenges.

English Language Arts

Determine Theme and Summarize Text
Reading: Literature

Strategy While reading, identify the main idea and then details that support the main idea. Underline the main idea and details or write them down. Use them to summarize the story.

3. Write the sentence that supports the theme with Luisa's actions.

_____

_____

_____

_____

4. Which action in the story best demonstrates the theme?

(A) Luisa cleans out Goldie's stall and feeds her.

(B) Marla pushes Luisa to help at the therapy center.

(C) The trainer ensures that Luisa works with a little horse.

(D) Luisa's parents set a good example by volunteering in the community.

5. Which detail from the story must be included in a clear and complete summary?

(A) The little horse's name is Goldie.

(B) Marla is comfortable working with horses.

(C) Luisa decides to volunteer despite her fears.

(D) People healing from accidents may use equine therapy.

Test Tip

Include only the important plot points and major characters in the summary of a story. Leave out less important characters and details the author includes to enhance the story.

6. Which character should be included in a complete summary of the story? Choose all that apply.

(A) Goldie's trainer

(B) Luisa's parents

(C) Luisa

(D) Marla

Write how you know.

_____

_____

_____

_____

7. Is Goldie important to mention in a summary? Explain why or why not.

_____

_____

_____

_____

8. Write a summary of the events in "Pot o' Gold."

_____

_____

_____

_____

_____

_____

English Language Arts

Understand Figurative Language
Reading: Literature

DIRECTIONS: Read the lines from "I'm Nobody." Then, answer the questions.

I'm Nobody *by Emily Dickinson*

I'm nobody! Who are you?

Are you nobody, too?

Then, there's a pair of us – don't tell!

They'd banish us, you know.

How dreary to be somebody!

How public like a frog

To tell your name the livelong day

To an admiring bog!

Strategy Identify the meaning of figurative language and use it to bring more meaning to stories and poems.

Test Tip Figurative language includes words and phrases that have meanings beyond their literal meanings. Similes use a comparison word, such as *like* or *as*. Use these words as clues to identify and interpret similes.

1. **Part A: The poet says that the public, or people, are like frogs. What type of figurative language is this an example of?**

   (A) simile

   (B) metaphor

   (C) idiom

   (D) proverb

   Part B: Which sentence best explains your answer to Part A?

   (A) The words used make sense if taken literally.

   (B) There is a message or theme about life and its meaning.

   (C) A metaphor compares two unlike things to make a strong point.

   (D) A simile compares two seemingly unlike ideas using the words *like* or *as*.

2. **Azim is writing a story about a baseball player who must make a choice. Should he stay in the minor leagues, where he is a star? Or should he move up to the major leagues? Choose the idiom that best describes what would happen if the character chooses to stay in the minor leagues.**

   (A) He would have bigger fish to fry.

   (B) He would be like a fish out of water.

   (C) He would be a big fish in a small pond.

   (D) He would be fishing in troubled waters.

   Write how you know.

   _____

   _____

   _____

   _____

English Language Arts

Understand Figurative Language
Reading: Literature

DIRECTIONS: Read the lines from "Paul Revere's Ride." Then, answer the questions that follow.

From "Paul Revere's Ride"
by Henry Wadsworth Longfellow

And the meeting-house windows, blank and bare,
Gaze at him with a spectral glare
As if they already stood aghast[1]
At the bloody work they would look upon.

[1] *aghast*—horrified

Strategy While reading, find the meaning of figurative language by asking yourself which characters, events, or ideas are being compared.

Test Tip Remember that metaphors, similes, and personification all compare seemingly different things to show how they are alike. First, identify what things are being compared. Then, ask: *What do these things have in common?*

3. **What type of figurative language appears in these lines?**

_____

_____

How do you know?

_____

_____

_____

_____

_____

_____

DIRECTIONS: Read "Fog." Then, answer the question that follows.

Fog *by Carl Sandberg*

The fog comes
on little cat feet.

It sits looking
over harbor and city
on silent haunches
and then moves on.

4. **Identify at least two ways that the fog is like a cat. Then, write a final sentence about how the comparison helps you understand or imagine fog better.**

_____

_____

Compare Characters, Settings, and Events
Reading: Literature

DIRECTIONS: Read the story. Then, answer the questions.

Strategy | As you read, ask yourself *Who? What? Where? When? How?* and *Why?* questions. These details will help you compare characters, settings, and events.

Test Tip | Read all parts of the question first.

Dark's for Sleeping

[1] BLAM!

[2] Hayden jumped up from the sofa. [3] The storm rolling overhead had provided a lightning and thunder extravaganza, but this noise was different. [4] "Sounds like that bolt got the transformer," Dad said, handing Hayden a flashlight. [5] "I suspect that we and our neighbors will be doing without power for a while, so we might as well turn in. [6] As Grandpa Dale likes to say, dark's for sleeping!"

[7] When Hayden woke in the morning, he heard Dad talking to Mom on the cell phone. [8] "I'm sure you're enjoying lots of electricity at the conference," he teased. [9] "No, don't worry about us. [10] We're fine. [11] See you when you get back!" [12] Dad hung up and turned to Hayden. [13] "The utility company reports that about six thousand homes are without power, and it'll probably be tomorrow before the damage is fixed."

[14] Hayden glowered. [15] He'd planned a perfect summer vacation day—playing video games, texting with friends, watching a favorite movie, and baking a homemade pizza. [16] "Oh, great—now I'll be bored all day," he whined.

[17] "Not necessarily," his dad said. [18] "Just ask yourself: What would Grandpa Dale have done on a summer's day when he was about your age? [19] No one in the little Oklahoma town where he grew up had electricity, ever."

[20] "I guess," Hayden said, trying to recall his grandfather's stories.

* * * * *

[21] Twelve-year-old Dale settled onto the dusty porch with a sigh and a long stretch and watched the sun drop behind the grain silo. [22] Summer vacation wasn't much of a vacation for a farm boy. [23] Mostly, it meant more chores and less quiet time to read and study, with just a bit of time left over for playing with his three brothers and three sisters. [24] Dale flexed his arms and legs and felt the satisfying soreness that follows a day well spent at work. [25] The chores were quickly transforming his skinny, boyish frame into that of a young man. [26] Now that dinner was cooked, eaten, and cleaned up, and now that the animals were fed and bedded down for the night and the laundry brought in from the line, Dale and his siblings could light the lanterns and enjoy some games while his parents chatted.

[27] The sun sank, taking with it the worst of the heat, and night insects began to chirr and whirr—a restful and welcome sound. [28] "Come on, Dale," called Darren, his older brother. [29] "Time for cards!" [30] The children played simple card games so that even the youngest sibling could have fun—and occasionally win. [31] Then, Darren took out Great Expectations, the Dickens novel they'd been reading, and read two chapters aloud. [32] By then, the younger children were yawning and rubbing their eyes, worn out by chores and heat and Darren's droning voice.

Compare Characters, Settings, and Events
Reading: Literature

[33] "Dark's for sleeping," Mama reminded them softly, and she and Papa went inside to their room. [34] The three girls went to their cots in the family room, and the four brothers laid out pallets on the screened porch—they had the best of the sleeping arrangements, they thought, because whatever breezes blew cooled the porch more than the house. [35] A bit of joking around and "Move your big, smelly feet because mine go there!" went on before sleep settled in. [36] Another day of work awaited.

* * * * *

[37] "Wow, what a different way to grow up," Hayden thought that evening, as he rummaged about the closet, directing the flashlight's beam toward where he was searching for a deck of cards. [38] He brought the deck into the den and held it up for his dad to see.

[39] "Are you thinking what I'm thinking?" Dad said.

[40] "Yep. You get the tent, and I'll get the sleeping bags." [41] In no time, they'd set up camp in the backyard, tying back the tent flap to catch the cool winds that the storm left behind when it finally rolled away to the south. [42] In the light of a halogen lantern, Dad shuffled the cards, and they talked contentedly about the coming school year. [43] Soon, Dad yawned. "I'm ready to call it a day," he said, stretching out on his bag.

[44] Just then, the lights flashed on in the house, and they heard the air conditioner grumble as it started to cool the stuffy rooms. [45] "What do you think?" Dad asked.

[46] Hayden smiled, thinking of Grandpa Dale on the porch. [47] "Dark's for sleeping," he said, zipping the tent door closed and shutting his eyes.

Strategy Make a character web to organize what the character says, what the character does, and how the character feels. Repeat the process for other characters in the story and then compare the webs.

Test Tip To learn about characters, find details about how they act, what they say and think, how they look, and what others say and do around them.

1. **Part A: In what way are the characters Hayden and Dale similar, according to the story's details?**

   (A) Both like to have close contact with their friends.

   (B) Both work hard during their summer school breaks.

   (C) Both enjoy spending time with their brothers and sisters.

   (D) Both find ways to make the best of challenging situations.

Part B: Which details from the story support this comparison? Choose three.

   (A) Hayden planned to bake a homemade pizza.

   (B) Dale sees that farm chores are making him strong and tough.

   (C) Dale and Hayden are both about the same age during their stories.

   (D) Hayden enjoys camping out in the backyard and visiting with his dad.

   (E) Dale is glad that the boys have to sleep on the porch rather than in the house.

English Language Arts

Compare Characters, Settings, and Events
Reading: Literature

Strategy While reading, identify all settings in a story to understand why characters do what they do. Stories often have events that happen in more than one setting.

Strategy A story's setting includes details about where the story is set—the place, objects, the way people dress, and even sounds and smells. Settings also include details about the time—the year or period during which events occur, the season, and the time of day.

2. **Which statement is true, as far as the story reveals, of all the characters?**

   (A) They enjoy the company of family.

   (B) They expect to work hard each day.

   (C) They prefer playing cards to reading.

   (D) They tell stories of their younger days.

3. **What sound mentioned in the story might be heard in the setting of Hayden's story but not in the setting of Dale's story?**

   (A) the shuffling of cards before a game

   (B) the "grumble" of the air conditioner

   (C) the sound of family members talking

   (D) the "whirr and chirr" of insects at night

4. **Explain how settings change from the paragraph that ends with sentence 20 and the paragraph that begins with sentence 21.**

   _____

   _____

   _____

   _____

5. **Complete the chart with details from the passage. Underline the details that both settings share.**

	Hayden's Setting	Dale's Setting
Describe the environment.		
Describe the things that provide entertainment.		
Describe the places characters live and work.		
Describe the time during which the characters live.		

Test Tip
To organize a story's events, record the events that form the beginning, middle, and end of the story. You can also record the events that introduce the problem in a story, develop that problem, and then resolve that problem.

English Language Arts

Compare Characters, Settings, and Events
Reading: Literature

Strategy   As you read, make inferences about what the characters think of each other. Base these inferences on not only what they say and do, but also on what you already know from your own experience.

6. Which statement about a problem that must be solved is supported by the story?

(A) Hayden's plans are spoiled by a strong summer storm.

(B) Dale's family has a hard time enduring the summer heat.

(C) Hayden and Dale find the routine of summer days boring.

(D) Hayden's mother is away at a conference during a power outage.

7. Which two sentences are evidence that Hayden no longer feels concerned about the power outage?

(A) Sentence 20

(B) Sentence 37

(C) Sentence 44

(D) Sentence 47

8. Hayden's dad is a positive, happy person. Is this a fair inference to make? Explain why or why not.

_____

_____

_____

_____

_____

9. Which inference is supported in the ending of the story?

(A) The power outage helped Hayden become closer to his grandfather.

(B) Hayden's dad was very worried and unhappy about the power outage.

(C) Spending time outdoors is something that was only done in the past.

(D) Electricity is the most important technology we have today.

10. Characters from three generations have roles in the story. Use details from the story to describe what Hayden learns from other characters.

_____

_____

_____

_____

_____

_____

_____

_____

_____

Explain Text Structure
Reading: Literature

DIRECTIONS: Read the excerpt from Act 1 of a play based on Charles Dickens' novel *A Christmas Carol*, and then, answer the questions.

The Money-Lender and His Clerk

Players:
  Scrooge, a wealthy money-lender
  Cratchit, a poor office clerk
  Fred, Scrooge's nephew
  Two charitable gentlemen

The time and place: London, in the 1840s, in the winter; Scrooge's office

CRATCHIT: *(meekly)* Mr. Scrooge, it's so cold. Why, the ink in my ink well is growing crystals! I could work much faster and better if the room were just a bit warmer. Might I—

SCROOGE: *(sternly but without looking up from his work)* Mr. Cratchit! Do you wish to remain in my employ this year, or would you prefer to spend the day standing in the wind, begging for your living?

CRATCHIT: *(even more meekly)* As you say, sir. *(He shivers as he speaks.)* You're right, of course, sir.

(Fred enters and shuts the door quickly behind him; even so, a frigid gust of wind and a sprinkling of snow accompany him into the gloomy little office.)

FRED: *(cheerily)* Greetings of the holiday to you, dear Uncle! *(He rubs his hands briskly.)* Though, I can't say "warmest greetings"—I almost think it's colder in your office than in the street!

SCROOGE: *(exasperated, throwing down his pen)* And now two of you harass me about the coal! Coal costs money, as you may have heard, and I don't choose to spend my hard-earned money on luxuries like hot air. Dress more warmly, Cratchit, as I do—take my example.

FRED: *(chuckling)* But, Uncle, I can't see how poor Bob could put on another layer of clothing and still move freely enough to wield his pen. However that may be, I can stay only a moment to offer my yearly invitation to dinner at my home tomorrow. You've never even met my delightful wife, Clara!

(Scrooge draws breath to scold Fred about the expense of getting married when the door swings open again, and two gentlemen cough their way into the room, choking on the cold air.)

Explain Text Structure
Reading: Literature

Strategy   Use structural elements of a drama to draw out more meaning.

Test Tip   Characters and setting are often identified before the play's lines start. Dialogue markers tell who is speaking. Stage directions—descriptions of what characters do and how they move and speak—are often in italics and inside parentheses.

1. **What do the stage directions suggest about the personality of Mr. Cratchit?**

   (A) He is a clever man who does well as a clerk.

   (B) He is a quiet man who finds his employer intimidating.

   (C) He is a sorrowful man who prefers a cold and dark room.

   (D) He is a cheerful man who likes his employer despite his grumpy ways.

2. **Write the stage direction that helps readers most clearly imagine the weather in which this action takes place.**

   _____

   _____

   _____

3. **What detail can readers find in the story structure that makes Scrooge's refusal to burn coal to heat the room even more confusing?**

   (A) The list of players says that Scrooge is wealthy.

   (B) Fred closes the office door to keep the cold out.

   (C) Fred's second speech suggests that Cratchit is already bundled up.

   (D) The description of the setting gives the place and time as 1840s London.

Test Tip   Make inferences about the characters based not only on what they say, but also on what the stage directions suggest about how they say it and what they do.

4. **If you were directing this scene, you would give instructions to the actors on how to play each role. Review the scene. Then, write notes to the actor playing Scrooge on what facial expressions he should use, how he should move, and how he should say each line. Draw on the structure of the play to support your instructions.**

   _____

   _____

   _____

   _____

   _____

   _____

   _____

   _____

   _____

   _____

   _____

English Language Arts

Analyze a Poem
Reading: Literature

DIRECTIONS: Read the poem. Then, answer the questions.

The Rainy Day *by Henry Wadsworth Longfellow*

The day is cold, and dark, and dreary;
It rains, and the wind is never weary;
The vine still clings to the mouldering[1] wall,
But at every gust the dead leaves fall,
And the day is dark and dreary.

My life is cold, and dark, and dreary;
It rains, and the wind is never weary;
My thoughts still cling to the mouldering Past,
But the hopes of youth fall thick in the blast,
And the days are dark and dreary.

Be still, sad heart! and cease repining[2];
Behind the clouds is the sun still shining;
Thy fate is the common fate of all,
Into each life some rain must fall,
Some days must be dark and dreary.

[1]*mouldering*—crumbling; decaying
[2]*repining*—complaining

Strategy Use structural elements of a poem to draw out more meaning. Although poems are shorter and have a unique format, they often have the same elements as fiction—characters, problems or conflict, setting, and theme.

Test Tip Whether you read a story or a poem, you can often identify a conflict and a resolution by asking these questions: *What does the speaker or character want that he can't get? How does the speaker either get the thing he wants or decide to do without it?*

1. **Which statement summarizes the conflict and resolution in the poem?**

   (A) The speaker is annoyed because the day is rainy until he sees the sun come out again.

   (B) The speaker is upset that his house's walls need repairing until he realizes he can fix them.

   (C) The speaker is sad about getting older until he remembers that everyone has sad days.

   (D) The speaker is enjoying the cool autumn weather until he remembers that summer will come soon.

2. **Part A: Which phrase describes the poem's tone in the first two stanzas?**

   (A) alarmed and restless

   (B) irritated and confused

   (C) thoughtful and content

   (D) gloomy and distressed

Analyze a Poem
Reading: Literature

Strategy Reread a story or poem and focus on the descriptive details to form a picture in your mind.

Test Tip Paying attention to details in a poem and visualizing those details will help you focus on the tone of the poem.

Part B: Which sentence in the third stanza marks a change in tone?

(A) "Behind the clouds is the sun still shining"

(B) "Thy fate is the common fate of all"

(C) "Into each life some rain must fall"

(D) "Some days must be dark and dreary"

3. **How does the title of the poem "The Rainy Day" fit with the tone?**

(A) it describes sunny weather

(B) it tells who the narrator is

(C) it describes a dreary, rainy day

(D) it tells what the poem is about

4. **Which words and phrases show how the narrator, or speaker, feels?**

_____

_____

5. **How would the poem be different if the poet described a bright, sunny day? Think about meaning, tone, and mood.**

_____

_____

_____

_____

Test Tip

When a story or poem includes visuals, such as drawings, the visuals usually serve a purpose. Examine the illustrations to analyze how they support, extend, or explain something about the setting, characters, or plot of the story or poem.

6. **Imagine you are an artist who is asked to create two illustrations for this poem. Describe the illustrations you would create to capture the tone of the poem. Explain how the illustrations would support, extend, or explain something about the poem's setting, speaker, or conflict.**

_____

_____

_____

_____

_____

_____

_____

_____

_____

English Language Arts

Understand Point of View
Reading: Literature

DIRECTIONS: Read the story. Then, answer the questions.

Four Thoughts

[1] One frigid afternoon in March, when spring was overdue and winter continued to reign, I spotted two silver dollars shining in a half-melted snowbank. [2] Instantly, I recalled stories of buried treasure I'd read when I was little. [3] So, I yanked off my gloves to dig through the snow, searching for more coins. [4] All I got for my trouble were two really cold hands. [5] I slipped the two coins in my pocket and went home much colder but a little richer.

[6] The next morning, as I walked to Tyler's house, I saw Megan and her little sister searching snowbanks. [7] I could guess why. [8] *Finders keepers* was my first thought. [9] I didn't need to add the *losers weepers* part of the rhyme because Moira was already crying for real.

[10] "I dropped them right here," she said through her tears. [11] Her gloveless hands were red from sifting through snow.

[12] "Maybe they got shoved down the street by the snow plow," Megan said optimistically. [13] "Let's try over there."

[14] My second thought was *They'll never know*. [15] I walked on past the girls toward Tyler's end of the street, carefully avoiding their eyes. [16] It didn't work.

[17] "Hello, Phil. [18] I don't suppose you've found two silver dollars recently?" Megan called. [19] Moira looked up from the snowbank with hope bright in her eyes.

[20] "Coins?" I said, but my third thought was *Look innocent!*

[21] "Yes, Moira dropped two silver dollars somewhere around here yesterday. [22] They were a gift from our aunt, who collects coins."

[23] "Big, heavy coins," Moira sniffled. [24] "How will I ever tell her that I've lost them already?" [25] She brushed small shards of ice off her shivering hands and wiped the chilled tears from her cheeks. [26] Her eyes were as red as her hands. [27] I hesitated, but only for a moment. My fourth thought was *You know the right thing to do*. [28] So, I said, "As a matter of fact, I dug two coins out of that snowbank yesterday. [29] I wondered who might have lost them."

[30] Moira ran to me and gave me a bear hug. [31] "Oh, thank you, thank you!" she cried. [32] I couldn't help but smile, and I trudged on toward Tyler's house, a bit poorer but much happier.

Strategy

Determine point of view by identifying who is telling the story. Then, determine what the narrator knows and shares.

Test Tip

Look for these clues that a narrative is a first-person narrative: The character telling the story refers to herself as "I" and reveals her thoughts. Look for these clues that a narrative is a third-person narrative: The voice of the storyteller seems to come from outside the story and tells of events from that perspective, not as a character taking part in the story.

English Language Arts

Understand Point of View
Reading: Literature

Strategy

Take notes about what you know about each character and what they think or feel. Then compare what you know with what the narrator knows to identify first-person or third-person point of view.

Test Tip

The teller of the events is the narrator. A narrator may be a character in the story (first-person point of view) or the voice of someone outside the story (third-person point of view).

1. **Which point of view is used in "Four Thoughts"?**

_____

2. **In what ways does the passage reveal the point of view? Choose two.**

   (A) The narrator refers to himself as *I*.

   (B) The narrator reveals his thoughts.

   (C) The narrator observes but is outside the action.

   (D) The narrator must guess what other characters think.

3. **Why does the writer use italicized words in sentences 8, 9, 14, and 27?**

   (A) to explain how the narrator plans to slip past the girls

   (B) to suggest that the narrator stole the coins from Moira

   (C) to set off the narrator's thoughts about keeping the coins

   (D) to show that the narrator is aware of how upset the sisters are

4. **What does the narrator of "Four Thoughts" have in common with someone reading the story?**

   (A) Both agree that people should behave honestly.

   (B) Both hope that more coins are hidden in the snowbank.

   (C) Both know all along that the narrator will give the coins back.

   (D) Both must use Moira's words and actions to infer what she thinks and feels.

5. **Read sentences 6, 7, 8, and 9 again. Then, rewrite them in a different point of view than the point of view in the story.**

_____

_____

_____

_____

_____

_____

_____

_____

_____

_____

_____

_____

English Language Arts

Compare Stories in the Same Genre
Reading: Literature

DIRECTIONS: Read the stories. Then, answer the questions.

How Did Things Come to Be?

Walks All Over the Sky

[1] Back when the sky was completely dark, there was a chief with two sons: a younger son, One Who Walks All Over the Sky, and an older son, Walking About Early. [2] The younger son was sad to see the sky always so dark, so he made a mask out of wood and pitch (the sun) and lit it on fire. [3] Each day, he travels across the sky. [4] At night, he sleeps below the horizon, and when he snores, sparks fly from the mask and make the stars. [5] The older brother became jealous. [6] To impress their father, he smeared fat and charcoal on his face (the moon) and makes his own path across the sky.

—From the Tsimshian of the Pacific Northwest

The Porcupine

[7] Once, Porcupine and Beaver argued about the seasons. [8] Porcupine wanted five winter months. [9] He held up one hand and showed his five fingers. [10] He said, "Let the winter months be the same in number as the fingers on my hand." [11] Beaver said, "No," and held up his tail, which had many cracks or scratches on it. [12] He said, "Let the winter months be the same in number as the scratches on my tail." [13] They argued more, and Porcupine got angry and bit off his thumb. [14] Then, holding up his hand with the four fingers, he said, "There must be only four winter months." [15] Beaver was afraid and gave in. [16] For this reason, today porcupines have four claws on each foot.

—From the *Tahltan: Teit, Journal of American Folk-Lore*, xxxii, 226

Strategy
Compare and contrast stories in the same genre to learn more about the genre.

Test Tip
The word *genre* means "kind" or "type." When you read to identify genre, ask: *What kind of story is this? Does it tell about things that could actually happen now (realistic fiction) or could have happened in the past (historical fiction)? Does it tell about things that could not happen now but might happen in the future or in another world (science fiction)? Does it include beings that are fantastic (fantasy)? Does it tell about nature or explain how things came to be (myth)?*

1. **What does the story "Walks All Over the Sky" explain?**
   A why brothers don't agree
   B ways fathers help sons
   C the start of stars, sun, and moon
   D the beginning of fire

2. **What does the story "The Porcupine" explain?**
   A how beavers' tails work
   B the length of winter
   C why animals argue
   D the purpose of summer

Compare Stories in the Same Genre
Reading: Literature

Fiery Pele

[17] Sky and Earth had six daughters and seven sons. [18] One daughter, Pele, earned another name, "woman who devours the land," because of her hot temper and because she both longed for and drove away her beloved. [19] Pele was born on an island heaved up from the sea, but after her sisters had had enough of her quarrelsome ways, her brother, king of the sharks, built a canoe for her to sail away. [20] Pele came at last to the islands of Hawaii, where she married the god of water. [21] But, her hot-headed nature and his constant motion clashed, and she drove him from the island, back into the sea, with streams of scalding lava. [22] Pele remained in the crater she created as her home. [23] Sometimes, though, she walks among the people, now as a lovely young woman, another time as a withered old woman. [24] And when she misses her husband of cool waves, or when she recalls past family arguments, she explodes in smoke, flame, and molten rock.

—Traditional Hawaiian myth

Test Tip
When comparing two stories in the same genre, look for the main message, or lesson, the characters learn. Then, look at details that show how the characters learned the lesson.

Test Tip
When comparing two stories, look at the characters, settings, and themes. Look for details that are the same, such as similar settings, and details that are different, such as actions characters take.

3. **What genre are these stories?**

   (A) myth

   (B) romance

   (C) realistic fiction

   (D) historical fiction

4. **What part of the natural world does each story explain?**

   Walks All Over the Sky: _____

   The Porcupine: _____

   Fiery Pele: _____

5. **What emotion explains the origin of the moon in "Walks All Over the Sky"?**

   (A) jealousy

   (B) happiness

   (C) sadness

   (D) boredom

6. **Why does Beaver agree to four winter months?**

   _____

   _____

7. **What feature in nature does the Pele, the daughter of Earth and Sky, represent?**

   (A) winter

   (B) the moon

   (C) a volcano

   (D) the night sky

   Write how you know.

   _____

   _____

Compare Stories in the Same Genre
Reading: Literature

8. How is the relationship among the main characters alike in all three stories?

(A) Jealousy or anger shapes the relationship.

(B) Love and admiration uphold the relationship.

(C) The relationship ends when the story ends.

(D) The relationship exists between human beings.

9. Are myths realistic fiction? Explain why or why not.

_____

_____

10. Which title would fit with the genre of the three stories you just read?

(A) The Life Cycle of a Butterfly

(B) How the Moon Pulled the Sun Down

(C) Two Sisters in the City

(D) Black Bears in Zoos

Write how you know.

_____

_____

11. Complete the chart to compare the plots of the three stories.

	How the problem or conflict begins	How the problem or conflict develops	How the problem or conflict ends
Walks All Over the Sky			
The Porcupine			
Fiery Pele			

Strategy

Use structure to describe a story's plot, including the conflict and how, or if, it is resolved.

Test Tip

Identify the beginning (when a problem or conflict is introduced), the middle (when the problem or conflict is developed), and the end (when the problem or conflict is solved or ended). Remember, not all conflicts are neatly resolved.

English Language Arts

Compare Stories in the Same Genre
Reading: Literature

12. **Which statement expresses a theme that each story supports?**

   Ⓐ Forceful action solves many problems.

   Ⓑ Family members forgive each other's faults.

   Ⓒ People have trouble living together in peace.

   Ⓓ The world of nature is full of unexplained mysteries.

   Write how you know.

   _____

   _____

13. **Stories such as these were often told to young listeners to teach a lesson about expected behavior. Choose one of the stories and explain the lesson you think young listeners might be expected to learn.**

   _____

   _____

   _____

   _____

   _____

   _____

   _____

   _____

14. **If you wrote a myth, which elements would you include? Choose all that apply.**

   Ⓐ characters

   Ⓑ features of nature

   Ⓒ a conflict

   Ⓓ realistic events

   Write how you know.

   _____

   _____

   _____

   _____

15. **How can comparing stories in the same genre help you understand the genre?**

   _____

   _____

   _____

   _____

   _____

   _____

   _____

   _____

Name _____ Date _____

Quote Text to Support Inferences
Reading: Informational Text

DIRECTIONS: Read the article. Then, answer the questions.

Assault of the Everlasting Jellies

[1] They're tiny—about the size of a little finger's fingernail. [2] They're soft—they'd be in trouble among pedestrians. [3] Yet, a species of sea life nicknamed "immortal jellyfish" is making its move on the world's oceans. [4] The scientific name of this creature is a mouthful: *Turritopsis dohrnii*.

[5] If that name sounds a little like "topsy-turvy," it fits. [6] These jellies are highly successful in the ocean for several reasons. [7] First, they traverse distances quickly, perhaps attached to cargo ships' hulls or floating inside the ballast water that helps keep ships upright. [8] Second, they adapt to new environments quickly. [9] For example, these jellies grow different numbers of tentacles in different water temperatures.

[10] However, their most amazing survival trick is what earns them the nickname "immortal." [11] When under stress—when there's not enough food or another hazard arises—every cell in an adult jelly transforms into a younger version of itself. [12] That's right: These jellies can age backward into the blobs from which they were born. [13] Colonies of these jelly blobs, or cysts, can then spawn hundreds of new jellies, each essentially a copy of the blob that spawned it. [14] Scientists are studying how these jellies' genes switch on and off. [15] In the meantime, swarms of the highly successful creatures float the world's oceans, reproducing as they go.

Strategy Make inferences by using facts from the passage and information you already know. Put the two together to create a new idea.

Test Tip Use details from the text to support inferences.

1. **Which sentence from the passage supports the inference that the jellies' ability to "age backward" is rare among living things?**

   Ⓐ Sentence 3, which explains why their nickname is "immortal jellyfish"

   Ⓑ Sentence 5, which says that their scientific name "sounds a little like 'topsy-turvy'"

   Ⓒ Sentence 10, which calls this ability a "most amazing survival trick"

   Ⓓ Sentence 15, which shows that this ability has led to "swarms of the highly successful creatures"

2. **Which sentence could be quoted to support the inference that a creature's ability to adapt to new surroundings affects whether it lives or dies?**

   Ⓐ Sentence 6

   Ⓑ Sentence 9

   Ⓒ Sentence 13

   Ⓓ Sentence 14

English Language Arts

Quote Text to Support Inferences
Reading: Informational Text

Strategy | Make inferences by identifying the main idea of the passage. Then, think about what you already know about the topic.

Test Tip | It is important to use details exactly as they appear in the passage to support an inference. Read the passage carefully.

3. **Which word from the passage describes a kind of motion and comes from a Latin prefix meaning "across" and a Latin root meaning "to turn"?**

    Ⓐ traverse, in Sentence 7

    Ⓑ tentacles, in Sentence 9

    Ⓒ transforms, in Sentence 11

    Ⓓ colonies, in Sentence 13

4. **Which sentence from the passage tells the meaning of *adapt* in sentence 8?**

    Ⓐ Sentence 7

    Ⓑ Sentence 9

    Ⓒ Sentence 11

    Ⓓ Sentence 13

    Write how you know.

    _____

    _____

    What does *adapt* mean?

    _____

    _____

Test Tip | When looking for context clues, read for words or phrases that may rename, explain, or define the word you don't know.

5. **Which phrases in the context surrounding the words "spawn" and "spawned" (Sentence 13) renames or defines a biological activity and provides a clue to the meaning of "spawn"? Choose all that apply.**

    Ⓐ "when there's not enough food"

    Ⓑ "from which they were born"

    Ⓒ "each essentially a copy of the blob"

    Ⓓ "how these jellies' genes switch on and off"

    Ⓔ "reproducing as they go"

Strategy | After you make an inference, reread the passage to identify details that clearly support the inference.

6. **A reader has made this inference after reading "Assault of the Everlasting Jellies":** *Swarms of these jellyfish are spreading through the oceans and threatening marine ecosystems.* **Does the passage support this inference? Explain your answer.**

    _____

    _____

    _____

    _____

    _____

    _____

    _____

English Language Arts

Summarize Using Main Ideas and Details
Reading: Informational Text

DIRECTIONS: Read the passage. Then, answer the questions.

Like No One Else's

[1] Fans of cop shows on television know the drill: When investigators arrive at the crime scene, they are careful not to touch anything. [2] Wearing gloves, they move gingerly around the room, dusting with powder to find fingerprints. [3] If they find prints on a weapon, they are relieved. [4] If they can match the fingerprints to those stored in a database, they may know who committed the crime.

[5] People have known for centuries that fingerprints are unique to individuals. [6] Not even identical twins have matching fingerprints. [7] The ridges, whorls, and loops that mark our fingers (and toes) belong to each of us alone. [8] And, with the exception of scars, our fingerprints remain the same our whole lives.

[9] In the past, fingerprints and palm prints were used as signatures, especially important in past times when only a few people needed to learn to read and write. [10] Historians have even found some artworks marked with their creator's prints. [11] However, it was not until the late 1880s that fingerprints were first matched with people in criminal cases, and even then, progress was slow. [12] It's one thing to know that each person's prints identify him or her. [13] It's another to build files of prints to check against prints found at a crime scene.

[14] In 1924, the United States Congress set up a section of the Federal Bureau of Investigation to collect and file fingerprints. [15] For decades, they were kept on cards, and in fact, several hundred million fingerprint cards are still on file with the FBI. [16] Today, computer databases have made matching fingerprints much easier and faster.

Strategy Use structure to summarize a passage. Identify a main idea for each paragraph of an informational passage. Then, list these main ideas to create a quick outline. Use your outline to summarize.

1. **Which statement best states the main idea of the entire passage?**
   (A) Fingerprints once served as signatures.
   (B) Millions of fingerprints are on file in this country.
   (C) Fingerprints can be used to identify individuals.
   (D) Toe prints and palm prints are also unique to individuals.

2. **Which statement best states the main idea of the second paragraph?**
   (A) Twins don't have matching fingerprints.
   (B) Fingerprints remain the same our whole lives.
   (C) In the past, fingerprints were used as signatures.
   (D) Fingerprints are unique to individuals.

Summarize Using Main Ideas and Details
Reading: Informational Text

Strategy Use the main idea to determine which details to include in a summary. Only include details that directly support the main idea.

3. **Part A: In the past, why were fingerprints not used to solve crimes?**

   (A) Files of prints for reference did not exist.

   (B) People did not know that fingerprints are unique.

   (C) People preferred to use palm prints for identification.

   (D) Only a few people needed to know how to read and write.

   Part B: Which sentences in the passage include details that support the answer to Part A? Choose three.

   (A) Sentence 5

   (B) Sentence 9

   (C) Sentence 11

   (D) Sentence 13

   (E) Sentence 16

4. **Reread Sentence 1. Why are investigators "careful not to touch anything" as they work on the crime scene?**

   (A) to avoid leaving their own fingerprints on evidence

   (B) to find new fingerprints to add to the databases and card files

   (C) to expedite the process of matching fingerprints to individuals

   (D) to keep from being injured while moving around the crime scene

Test Tip

When you summarize an informational passage, include a main idea for each paragraph and transitional words to link those ideas logically. Leave out examples, details, quotations of experts, and other supporting materials.

5. **Write a summary of the passage. Include the main ideas and transitions that link those ideas.**

   _____

   _____

   _____

   _____

   _____

   _____

   _____

   _____

   _____

   _____

   _____

   _____

English Language Arts

Connect Text and Visuals
Reading: Informational Text

DIRECTIONS: Read the paragraph, and study the chart. Then, answer the questions.

[1] As a beginning player, you may be wondering, "Why do I have to learn a bunch of terms? [2] I just want to play!" [3] The answer is simple: because your coach will use these terms during practice. [4] When the coach yells, "Slide your hand on the grip toward the butt," you won't know what to do if you don't know where the butt of the racket is. [5] Also, learning these terms will help you understand how the racket works. [6] Even a beginner can guess that it is more effective to make contact between the ball and the sweet spot than between the ball and the dead spot. [7] Therefore, knowing these terms will help you grasp the physics of the game. [8] They help you grasp why one spot on the racket gives you a fast or floating shot and why another puts a spin on the ball. [9] And, yes, you need to learn the terms because there will be a quiz later.

Term	Definition
face	the oval-shaped area of strings framed by metal or wood
grip	the handle—usually wrapped with leather or plastic
butt	the bottom of the handle
sweet spot	the area on the face that delivers the greatest momentum to the ball
dead spot	the area on the face that delivers the least momentum to the ball
center of mass	the balance point of the racket, usually in the neck between the face and the grip

Strategy

When a passage includes a graphic, study the graphic and any labels before you read the passage. Then, as you read the passage, glance back at the graphic to match terms that appear both on the graphic and in the passage.

Test Tip

Graphics and diagrams often include technical language. The illustration can help you understand what technical terms mean. If you use these terms in a written response to a test item, check their spelling against the graphic's labels.

English Language Arts

Connect Text and Visuals
Reading: Informational Text

Strategy Connect visuals to the text and determine how they relate to each other. Does the visual show information already in the text? Or, does it give new information?

Test Tip Some visuals include titles. Use the titles as a clue to the kind of information presented in the visual.

1. **According to the passage, for what reasons should a player study the chart? Choose three.**

   (A) to be able to respond to the coach's guidance

   (B) to teach beginning players the parts of the racket

   (C) to compare the tennis racket to a racquetball racket

   (D) to know what part of the racket the ball should strike

   (E) to understand how the racket and the ball interact during play

2. **Which terms in the chart help a player understand the racket's shape by comparing it to another familiar form? Choose three.**

   (A) butt

   (B) face

   (C) grip

   (D) dead spot

   (E) sweet spot

3. **Study the chart. If a coach directed a player to "slide your hand on the grip toward the butt," what action would the player take?**

   (A) The player would contact the ball with the racket's sweet spot.

   (B) The player would move her hand higher, toward the center of mass.

   (C) The player would move her hand lower, toward the bottom of the grip.

   (D) The player would hold the racket on top of the head and on the grip.

4. **Which title, if added to the chart, would most clearly connect the chart and the passage?**

   (A) The Tennis Racket

   (B) Get to Know Your Racket

   (C) The Physics of Ball Striking

   (D) Backhand and Forehand Grips

5. **Which signal words in the passage help readers understand the cause-effect relationship between studying the chart and learning to play tennis? Write two.**

   _____

   _____

Analyze Multiple Accounts
Reading: Informational Text

DIRECTIONS: Read the passages. Then, answer the questions.

Journal, February 10

[1] I did it! [2] Well, I sort of did it, anyway. [3] I didn't win first place, but I came in second. [4] I'm really proud of that. [5] At first, I was intimidated when I looked and saw all of those people seated in the cafeteria. [6] I was afraid I'd forget everything I'd learned. [7] But then, I reassured myself: "You studied hard. [8] You know all those words. [9] Come on—you can do it!" [10] My first word was *indicate*: i-n-d-i-c-a-t-e. [11] How basic can you get? [12] Spelling it correctly boosted my confidence. [13] Then, I knew I could handle the rest of the words, too. [14] The only word that stumped me was *cannibal*. [15] I spelled it c-a-n-n-i-b-l-e—oops. [16] Rebecca spelled it right, and she breezed through her last word: *hydraulics*. [17] Oh, well. [18] Still, I won a dictionary, and a reporter took a photograph of Rebecca and me for the county newspaper. [19] When I came home, my family had a party to celebrate my achievement and hard work! [20] I'm pleased for Rebecca, but tomorrow, I'll start studying for next year's contest.

Local Students Finish First, Second in Regional Spelling Bee

[21] Ben Hanson, age 12, of Park Creek, finished second in the Regional Spelling Bee sponsored by the Literacy Society. [22] He spelled eight words correctly, finally stumbling over the word *cannibal*. [23] Hanson won a new dictionary for his efforts. [24] Rebecca Cohen, 13, also of Park Creek, won first prize for spelling the word *hydraulics*. [25] She will receive a $100 savings bond and proceed to the National Spelling Bee held in Washington, D.C., next month. [26] Both students attend Mitchell Middle School, where they were coached by Mr. Tomás Perez, longtime language arts teacher.

Strategy   Read paired passages twice—once to understand each one by itself, and again to compare the information. Take notes on the second read, and write down what is alike and what is different.

Test Tip   Think about point of view, structure, and author's purpose as you compare passages, not just the details.

1. **Complete the chart to compare the two accounts of the spelling bee.**

	writer	purpose	audience
Journal, February 10			
Local Students Finish First, Second in Regional Spelling Bee			

English Language Arts

Analyze Multiple Accounts
Reading: Informational Text

Strategy Identify the passage's point of view and use it to evaluate the information presented.

Test Tip First-person accounts are those told by the person who experienced the events. First-person accounts usually share emotions and thoughts. Third-person accounts are written by people who were not part of the events. Third-person accounts usually offer facts.

2. **Which information on the topic is included only in the journal account of the spelling bee?**

   Ⓐ the winning word

   Ⓑ the word that Ben misspelled

   Ⓒ the prize for winning first place

   Ⓓ the way Ben feels about finishing second

Test Tip When you answer questions about the purpose of an account, describe the audience—the intended readers—to yourself before answering. Then, ask: *Does my answer take this audience into account?*

3. **Write one sentence from each account that most strongly supports the claim that Ben and Rebecca know each other as friends, as well as competitors.**

   _____

   _____

   _____

5. **Write a sentence that describes the tone of Ben's journal account. Then, write a sentence that describes the tone of the newspaper's account. Explain why each tone is appropriate for its style of writing.**

   _____

   _____

   _____

   _____

   _____

4. **Which sentences in Ben's account express his honest disappointment? Choose two.**

   Ⓐ "I did it!"

   Ⓑ "Well, I sort of did it, anyway."

   Ⓒ "I'm really proud of that."

   Ⓓ "Oh, well."

   Ⓔ "I'm pleased for Rebecca"

Compare Structure
Reading: Informational Text

DIRECTIONS: Read each paragraph. Then, answer the questions that follow.

[1] Wolfgang Amadeus Mozart was born on January 27, 1756, in Austria. [2] When he was just 3 years old, he learned to play the harpsichord. [3] He began composing music when he was 5 years old with the help of his father, who was also his teacher. [4] At age 6, he performed for the Empress of Austria. [5] The child Mozart astonished audiences with his musical talents. He was widely regarded as a child genius.

Strategy   Use clue words to identify passage structure.

Test Tip   Chronological passage structures often use temporal terms, such as *first*, *next*, and *finally*. Cause-and-effect structures often use transitions, such as *because*, *as a result*, and *therefore*.

1. **What passage structure does this paragraph share with many other biographies?**
   - (A) cause-effect
   - (B) chronological
   - (C) comparison
   - (D) problem-solution

   What clue words in the paragraph helped you identify its structure?

   _____

   _____

   _____

   _____

[1] By your third class, you wish you had twigs to prop your eyelids up. [2] Your head is nodding. [3] Then, you're facedown on your desk, at risk of drooling. [4] Clearly, you're not getting enough sleep. [5] Take action! [6] Go to bed 15 minutes earlier than usual each night until you can fall asleep an hour sooner than you do now. [7] (Be patient—this takes time!) [8] Make sure your room is dark—really dark—and cool. [9] You'll sleep better, and you won't sleep on your desk!

2. **Identify the passage structure and purpose of the paragraph.**
   - (A) cause-effect, to help readers study smarter
   - (B) problem-solution, to help readers sleep better
   - (C) chronological, to help readers understand sleep stages
   - (D) comparison, to help readers contrast feeling rested with feeling tired

   How do you know?

   _____

   _____

English Language Arts

Compare Structure
Reading: Informational Text

DIRECTIONS: Read each paragraph. Then, answer the questions that follow.

[1] Some people say that playing video games is a total waste of time. [2] Recent research, however, tells a different story. [3] Good game design encourages players to keep trying and not give up when facing challenges. [4] Tricky puzzles and complex landscapes foster memory skills. [5] These abilities may transfer to other activities, such as schoolwork—as long as the player eventually puts down the game controller and steps away from the console.

Strategy — As you read, identify the author's purpose for writing the passage to help you identify structure.

Test Tip — Purpose and structure are closely related. If two subjects are presented side by side, the purpose might be to compare and contrast them. If steps to a process are given, a problem and solution structure may be in use. Identify the purpose of the passages you read.

3. **Which statement describes the paragraph's story structure?**

   (A) It uses chronology to explain how to start a game.

   (B) It uses cause-effect to explain positive results of game playing.

   (C) It uses comparison to help readers choose the most challenging games.

   (D) It uses problem-solution to fix the issue of gamers spending too much time playing.

4. **Which phrase in the paragraph is a clue that the story structure is comparison?**

   (A) "If you have a choice" (Sentence 1)

   (B) "In a big city" (Sentence 2)

   (C) "on the other hand" (Sentence 3)

   (D) "a variety of fun activities" (Sentence 4)

5. **A friend asks you for advice on how to end an ongoing argument with her brother. Which story structure would you use to present your advice? Explain your choice.**

   _____

   _____

   _____

   _____

[1] If you have a choice about where to go on vacation, do you prefer the beach or a big city? [2] In a big city, you can visit museums, go to concerts, and try interesting foods. [3] The beach, on the other hand, offers the soothing sound of waves on the sand, the possibility of finding beautiful shells to take home, and plenty of time to swim. [4] Of course, you could visit a big city on a coast and enjoy a variety of fun activities.

English Language Arts

Determine the Meaning of Words and Phrases
Language

DIRECTIONS: Read the passage. Then, answer the questions.

Sleeping Like a Log

[1] Here's a word for you: homeostasis. [2] Homeostasis is a state in which an animal's body is neither too cool nor too hot, in which all systems are functioning as they should be for good health. [3] Animals, including humans, expend much energy keeping their bodies in this state of balance. [4] And, energy requires food intake.

[5] What happens, then, to animals that live in parts of the world where winter lasts a long time, reducing food supplies? [6] These animals have a hard time finding enough food to keep their body temperatures up against the cold. [7] They are in danger of freezing to death. [8] Some animals—many of them small mammals—have developed the ability to game the system, however. [9] When they cannot eat enough to stay warm, they snuggle into burrows, nests, or dens and sleep for weeks or even months!

Strategy — Find context clues in the same sentence as the word or phrase you want to understand. Also, look in the sentences that come before and after the word.

---

1. How does the sentence "And, energy requires food intake" help you determine the meaning of the word *expend* in Sentence 3?

   (A) Energy is required to eat food.

   (B) Energy is the same as food.

   (C) Food gives bodies energy to use.

   (D) Food is not important for energy.

2. Which phrase could replace the word *expend* in Sentence 3, based on the context of the first and second paragraphs?

   (A) take in

   (B) use up

   (C) reach out

   (D) depend on

3. Write the sentence that supports the idea that the author is concerned about animals surviving winter.

   _____

   _____

   _____

   _____

4. How does the title help you find meaning in the passage?

   _____

   _____

   _____

   _____

Determine the Meaning of Words and Phrases
Language

5. Which two phrases help you find the meaning of "keeping their bodies in this state of balance" in sentence 3?

(A) "keep their body temperatures up"

(B) "an animal's body is neither too cool nor too hot"

(C) "energy requires food intake"

(D) "all systems are functioning as they should be for good health"

Write how you know.

_____

_____

6. How do animals "game the system" in winter?

(A) They eat as much food as possible.

(B) They sleep for weeks to use less energy.

(C) They decrease their food intake earlier.

(D) They keep their bodies very cool.

Test Tip

When you encounter an unfamiliar word, check to see whether it has a familiar root or prefix. You might read the word *geosynchronous*, for example, and notice that it uses the prefix *geo-* and the root *-synch-*. If you know that *geo-* means "having to do with Earth" (geography, geological) and *-synch-* means "having to do with time" (out of synch), you can guess that the unfamiliar word might mean "in time with Earth." A geosynchronous satellite, in fact, moves around Earth at the same speed that Earth turns. It remains over the same spot on Earth while it is in orbit.

7. The Latin prefix *homeo-* means "same, similar," and the Greek root *-stasis-* means "standing still." Write a definition of the word *homeostatic* that draws on these word parts and on what you learned in the passage. Give an example of something that can be described as homeostatic.

_____

_____

_____

8. Read the title of the passage. Identify the type of figurative language the title uses, what the title means, and why it fits the content of the passage.

_____

_____

_____

_____

_____

_____

_____

_____

_____

_____

_____

_____

English Language Arts

Understand Word Relationships
Language

DIRECTIONS: Read the passage. Then, answer the questions.

Hibernation

[1] During a deep sleep, called *hibernation*, animals' body temperatures drop dramatically. [2] How, then, do they maintain homeostasis? [3] Biologists now understand that by lowering their body temperatures, these animals decrease their need for food. [4] The rate at which they burn energy drops. [5] To make this possible, the animals' systems slow down: heart rate drops, breathing slows, and brain activity gets sluggish. [6] In fact, if a predator finds the animal during hibernation, the hibernator is in jeopardy. [7] The animal cannot become alert quickly enough to flee.

[8] Hibernation is not a fool-proof method of making it through winter alive. [9] Animals must either eat enough in late summer and autumn to develop layers of fat to live on as they sleep, or stockpile food where they hibernate so that they can awaken randomly to eat. [10] If the animal is unsuccessful, then it may fall asleep and never wake up to see another spring.

Strategy   Look for clues to word relationships as you read. Look for synonyms and antonyms, in particular.

Test Tip   A synonym of a less familiar word expands your understanding of that word. An antonym helps you understand a less familiar word by stating what it does *not* mean.

1. **What information about hibernation would you likely find in a thesaurus?**

   (A) Other terms for *hibernation* include *torpor* and *brumation*.

   (B) Some biologists think that bears hibernate but others do not.

   (C) The word *hibernate* has, as its root, the Latin word for winter: *hiber*.

   (D) Some fish and reptiles also spend time in a state similar to hibernation.

2. **Which three facts from the passage support the claim in sentence 8 that hibernation is not a "fool-proof" way to survive a long winter?**

   (A) A stockpile of food may run out before spring arrives.

   (B) An animal may fail to eat enough food before hibernating.

   (C) An animal's body temperature may remain too high for it to sleep deeply.

   (D) A predator may find a hibernating animal and kill it before it can wake up.

3. **Write the meaning of the word *hibernation*.**

   _____

   _____

   Why do animals hibernate?

   _____

   _____

Understand Word Relationships
Language

4. **What does the word *flee* mean in sentence 7?**

(A) eat

(B) hide

(C) sleep

(D) run

Write how you know.

_____

_____

5. **Which phrase is more formal and direct in conveying the idea in Sentence 6, which is the hibernator "is in jeopardy"?**

(A) The animal will likely die.

(B) The animal will likely go back to sleep.

(C) The animal will likely wake up and eat.

(D) The animal will likely flee the nest or den.

6. **Write other words for *stockpile* using the context of the passage.**

_____

_____

7. **What does the word *sluggish* mean in sentence 5?**

(A) speedy

(B) warm

(C) slow

(D) fat

Write how you know.

_____

_____

_____

_____

_____

English Language Arts

Write an Opinion
Writing

Strategy State your opinion clearly. Then, support your opinion with reasons, facts, and examples to make it convincing.

Test Tip *Opinion*, *claim*, *stance*, and *position* are all words used for an idea that you have and believe to be right or true. You will sometimes see these words used interchangeably.

DIRECTIONS: Choose a topic about which you have a firm opinion. This opinion might be a change that you would like to see happen or a solution to a problem. Then, complete the chart to gather and organize the reasons you have the opinion, as well as facts and examples that support your opinion.

STEP 1: State your topic and your opinion about the topic.

My topic:

My opinion:

STEP 2: Gather support for your opinion.

Reasons I have my opinion:

Facts that support my opinion:

Examples that support my opinion:

STEP 3: Organize your writing. Give the reasons you hold the opinion first. Then, decide in what order to present supporting facts and examples. For example, you could place the strongest support last so that readers will remember it most. Add numbers if you want to include more support.

1.

2.

3.

STEP 4: Write a conclusion that explains how you hope your opinion will cause readers to respond.

My conclusion:

English Language Arts

Write an Opinion
Writing

DIRECTIONS: Read the opinion piece a student has written. Then, answer the questions.

Library Hours

[1] Students in our school face a real problem. [2] We have homework that we could do in the library, but the library does not stay open after school. [3] We need to use the books, computers, and Internet access that the library offers. [4] Many of us do not have these things at home. [5] How can we do well on our assignments without these resources?

[6] I asked our principal why the library is not open for a while after school, and he said the school cannot afford to pay the librarian to stay late. [7] I spoke with parents of the students in my class. [8] They said they would be willing to take turns staying after to make sure students use the library appropriately and help with homework. [10] This would cost the school nothing and also give parents a way to help students.

---

1. **Which kind of information would offer strong support for the writer's opinion if added to the first paragraph?**

   (A) lists of useful books on the library's shelves

   (B) the names of the school and the school's librarian

   (C) a table of hours that the library is open during the school day

   (D) examples of homework assignments that require library resources

2. **Which transition could link the actions in Sentences 6 and 7 logically to help readers follow the writer's ideas?**

   (A) First,

   (B) Then,

   (C) Even so,

   (D) On the one hand,

3. **Which statement, if inserted in the second paragraph, would show that the writer understands the principal's concern about keeping the library open?**

   (A) I feel that students should have access to the Internet from home.

   (B) I appreciate how much our librarian helps us during the school day.

   (C) I agree that the school must carefully budget and spend the money it has.

   (D) I know that teachers must spend time after the school day planning and grading.

4. **Write a short conclusion to the student's opinion paper in which you sum up his opinion and ask readers to take action.**

   _____

   _____

   _____

   _____

   _____

   _____

Test Tip

Often, when writers present their opinions, they conclude by encouraging readers to take a certain action or to think further about an idea.

English Language Arts

Write an Informative/Explanatory Text
Writing

DIRECTIONS: Read the passage in which a student explains how to make and stick to a budget. Then, answer the questions on the next two pages.

Your Budget Is Your Friend

[1] Always running out of money? [2] Have no idea where your money goes? [3] Saving for a special trip, activity, or object? [4] If you answered yes to any of these questions, it is time to plan a budget and stick to it. [5] Many people think budgets are too restrictive or too hard to follow. [6] A budget can be very simple, and understanding how to use one can help you save for special purchases or events. [7] Follow this method to create a livable budget:

[8] Record your spending habits. [9] Look at the money you spend. [10] Do you buy your lunch? [11] Do you buy a soft drink or even water from a machine? [12] You may discover you spend money foolishly. [13] Buying a candy bar for $0.50 every day may seem insignificant, but by the end of the month, it totals $15.00. [14] Instead, put a snack from home in your backpack.

[15] The next step is determining your debits and credits. [16] Look at what money comes in and what goes out. [17] If you determine your spending habits, you will know what your debits are. [18] Credits might be harder to determine if you do not have a job. [19] Determine all the ways you get money. [20] For example, count the dollars you earn or money given to you as presents. [21] How much each week do you have available to spend? [22] What are your sources of income? [23] If you do not have a regular source of income, you need to find ways to make money. [24] Do you have an allowance? [25] Can you negotiate with your family to raise your allowance? [26] Offer to do more chores or special jobs that will increase your income. [27] Remember, your debits should not be more than your credits.

[28] The last step is determining your cash flow and savings goals. [29] How much money do you have available each week to spend? [30] You might budget a small cash flow for yourself because you want to save for a new pair of skis, which means you might earn $10.00 a week but allow yourself to spend only $3.00. [31] Look at three important categories: [32] How much money do you wish to save? [33] How much money do you need for essentials? [34] How much money do you want for frivolous activities?

Write an Informative/Explanatory Text
Writing

Strategy

When you write to inform or explain, gather the facts you will present about a topic. Then, decide how to order the information. Cause-effect, sequence (time order), and compare-contrast are structures often used in informative and explanatory writing.

Test Tip

Informative writing provides accurate information about a topic that readers want or need to know about. Explanatory writing often connects pieces of information by showing causes and effects or problems and solutions.

1. **The writer uses words especially related to the topic of budgeting, such as** *debit* **and** *credit*. **Which revision of Sentence 9 uses another word especially related to the topic of budgeting while keeping the sentence's meaning the same?**

   (A) Look at your expenditures.
   (B) Look at the cash you spend.
   (C) Prices are something to look at.
   (D) Examine the money you spend.

2. **What structure did the student use to organize the information?**

   (A) space order
   (B) process order
   (C) order of importance
   (D) compare-contrast order

3. **Read Sentences 24, 25, and 26 again. Clear explanatory writing often includes examples to help readers understand ideas. Write one or two sentences that offer examples of how a reader could perform the instructions in these sentences.**

   _____

   _____

   _____

   _____

   _____

4. **Sentence 5 has a logical relationship to Sentence 6, but the writer did not used a transition to link these ideas. Which two transitions could the writer add to the beginning of Sentence 6 to explain how the two sentences relate?**

   (A) So,
   (B) Also,
   (C) In fact,
   (D) However,
   (E) As a consequence,

English Language Arts

Write an Informative/Explanatory Text
Writing

<table>
<tr>
<td>

Test Tip

Identify the relationship among the sentences. For example, does one build on the other? Does one explain the other? Does one contradict the other? Then, choose a transition—a word, phrase, or even sentence, that points out that relationship.

</td>
<td>

Test Tip

Review how the other paragraphs begin. Then, to make the structure more clear, write a new sentence that matches the first sentences of the other paragraphs and that fits the overall structure of the passage.

</td>
</tr>
</table>

5. **Which sentence should replace Sentence 8 at the beginning of the second paragraph to make the passage's structure more clear?**

  (A) You should record your spending habits.

  (B) Don't forget to record your spending habits.

  (C) The first step is to record your spending habits.

  (D) Recording your spending habits is an important task.

6. **Which resource would likely help readers who want to follow the steps of developing a basic budget?**

  (A) a book about saving for college costs

  (B) a website listing sale prices on skis

  (C) a bank brochure about opening a savings account

  (D) a chart in which income and expenses are tracked

7. **The last sentence of the passage contains a detail. This tells you that the student has left out the conclusion of the informative passage. Think about the goal of the passage. Then, write a one or two sentences to conclude the passage.**

_____

_____

_____

_____

_____

_____

English Language Arts

Write an Informative/Explanatory Text
Writing

DIRECTIONS: Write three paragraphs about how to make extra money for a special purchase or event, or about another goal that students your age may want to pursue. Include the following:

- An introduction that encourages readers to try your ideas
- Two ways to achieve the goal you write about
- Specific examples of steps to take toward the goal
- A clear order in which to take the steps

_____

_____

_____

_____

_____

_____

_____

_____

_____

_____

_____

_____

_____

_____

_____

_____

_____

_____

_____

_____

_____

_____

_____

_____

_____

_____

_____

_____

_____

English Language Arts

Write a Narrative
Writing

DIRECTIONS: Read a section of "Clever Grandmother Spider," a Native American legend, and then answer the questions.

> [1] The Peoples, both humans and animals, shivered in the dark in the early times. [2] No moon or stars spangled the night, so when the sun left the sky, the Peoples suffered. [3] A hawk brought news, one day, of the Eastern Peoples. [4] "They have a thing called fire," she insisted, "that gives warmth and light at night." [5] Opossum volunteered to go get some of this thing called fire, but the Eastern Peoples drove him away with a flaming branch that burned his tail. [6] Other brave animals tried, too, but none returned with the precious fire. [7] Grandmother Spider said, "I will bring the fire back." [8] The Peoples laughed. [9] How could so small a creature capture and bring back fire? [10] Grandmother Spider ignored them. [11] She took river clay and her own silk and formed a tiny pot. [12] Then, she walked for many days to find the fire where the Eastern Peoples lived. [13] They never saw her as she crept near the fire and slipped a single ember into her pot. [14] She turned to journey home.

Strategy Plan a narrative by thinking of how a story starts, how it develops, and how it ends. Use temporal words such as *next*, *then*, and *finally* to show the order of events.

Test Tip If you are asked to write an original story, prewrite first to identify a beginning that creates a problem, a middle that develops the problem, and an end that resolves the problem.

1. Read this sentence: "That is why Opossum's tail is bare to this day." Where in the plot does this detail make sense?

   Ⓐ after Sentence 4

   Ⓑ after Sentence 5

   Ⓒ after Sentence 8

   Ⓓ after Sentence 14

   Write how you know.

   _____

   _____

2. Which phrase could be added to be beginning of Sentence 7 to show how the problem remains?

   Ⓐ Sadly,

   Ⓑ At last,

   Ⓒ A while ago,

   Ⓓ In contrast,

3. Rewrite Sentence 14 so that readers can see in their minds how Grandmother Spider carried the fire as she journeyed home. Use descriptive details.

   _____

   _____

   _____

   _____

Write a Narrative
Writing

4. Sentences 8 and 9 describe the Peoples' reaction to Grandmother Spider's offer. Write a line or two of dialogue that Opossum might say to explain why the Peoples laugh.

_____

_____

5. This legend has a beginning that explains the problem—the cold, dark night. It has a middle that develops the problem—no animal is able to get the fire. The legend is missing an end that resolves the problem. Write an ending, based on the events so far, that shows how the problem is solved.

_____

_____

_____

_____

Strategy

Plan a narrative by choosing people, places, and events that will be in the story. Use an outline or other to keep your ideas organized and to make sure you have details.

Test Tip

Choosing the right words makes a narrative more interesting to read. Use exact words and phrases and figurative language.

DIRECTIONS: A narrative is a story that tells about real or imagined events. Write a narrative about the origin or beginning of something, such as an element in nature. It can be real or imagined. Write your paragraph on the lines. Your paragraph should have the following:

- A narrator and/or characters
- A natural sequence of events
- Dialogue
- Descriptions of actions, thoughts, and feelings
- Time words and phrases to show the order of events
- Concrete words and sensory details
- A sentence to end your paragraph

Understand Editing and Revising
Writing

DIRECTIONS: Read the report. Then, answer the questions.

Citizens Protest Tree Removal

[1] Planning for the new community center came to a sudden stop because of a tree. [2] A 60-year-old magnolia tree, to be exact. [3] For years, this tree provided shade for parents who brought their children to swim at the city pool. [4] Since the pool was closed and the new pool opened across town, parents have taken their children to that pool. [5] Now, the magnolia is "in the way" of the new community center, and city planners will announce their plans to cut it down.

[6] But, what they didn't expect was an outcry from citizens. [7] "This tree was a sapling when my grandmother was a girl in this city," said one citizen. [8] I refuse to let these people cut it down, just to make room for some new building! [10] Another protester said, "This tree is healthy. [11] It could live another 40 years. [12] Why chop down such a beautiful magnolia?"

[13] The city planners are taking the citizens' concerns seriously; they are considering building a courtyard around the tree. [14] The magnolia is the state tree of Mississippi and bears large flowers with a strong, sweet odor.

Strategy When you read to revise, make sure each paragraph of an informative passage has just one main idea. Find and remove details and examples that don't support the main idea.

Test Tip Revise to clarify your ideas and ensure your reader can understand your meaning.

1. **Which sentence in the first paragraph strays from the report's topic and should be removed?**

   (A) Sentence 2
   (B) Sentence 3
   (C) Sentence 4
   (D) Sentence 5

   Write how you know.

   _____

   _____

   _____

   _____

2. **Which three revisions to the third paragraph would strengthen the report's conclusion?**

   (A) Add an explanation about why the city pool had to be moved.
   (B) Add a new sentence with instructions on how to care for magnolias.
   (C) Include a quotation from a city planner responding to the citizens' concerns.
   (D) Add a description of what the courtyard might look like.
   (E) Remove the second sentence because it strays from the main idea.

Understand Editing and Revising
Writing

3. **Which correction should be made so that the tense of Sentence 5 is correct?**

   Ⓐ Change "is" to "was"

   Ⓑ Change "is" to "has been"

   Ⓒ Change "will announce" to "have announced"

   Ⓓ Change "will announce" to "will have announced"

Write how you know.

_____

_____

_____

4. **What change is needed so that Sentence 8 is correctly punctuated?**

   Ⓐ Add a comma after "people."

   Ⓑ Place the sentence in quotation marks.

   Ⓒ Change the comma after "down" to a period.

   Ⓓ Change the exclamation point to a question mark.

Write how you know.

_____

_____

_____

Test Tip

Revise to ensure that each sentence expresses a complete thought. Identify sentence fragments by checking that each sentence has a subject and verb that agree. If a sentence is missing either the subject or the verb, it is a fragment and should be revised.

5. **Sentence 2 is a fragment. It has a subject but no verb that agrees with the subject. Revise sentence 2 either by writing it as a complete sentence or by combining it with another sentence.**

_____

_____

_____

_____

_____

_____

_____

_____

_____

_____

_____

Strategy Review

DIRECTIONS: Each strategy below is followed by a review, a passage, and one or more questions. Use these to review important strategies.

Strategy Use details from the text to make inferences, understand themes, and draw out meaning.

A *theme* can be a lesson learned. Or, a theme can be an idea about what life is like or what people are like. *Theme* is a term used for fiction texts, but it is similar to the main idea in nonfiction texts. You won't often see a theme written out in a story. Details in the story will help you figure out the theme. Then, you can put it in your own words.

Cheerful Crawfish

Before the beginning, water was everywhere. But no earth, people, or animals were visible. There were birds, however, who held a council to decide if it might be best to have all land or all water. "Let us have land, so we can have more food," said some of the birds. Others said, "Let's have all water, because we like it this way."

So, they appointed Eagle as their Chief to decide one way or the other. Eagle decided upon land and asked, "Who will go and search for land?" Dove volunteered first and flew away. In four days, he completed his hunt and returned, reporting, "I could not find land anywhere." The birds complained gloomily. Where, now, would they live? If patient Dove couldn't find land, then no one could.

Crawfish came swimming along just then, and saw the birds' disappointment. At once he offered to help the council search for land. He disappeared under the water for four days. The birds waited a while, gave up, and flew off—except for Chief Eagle. When Crawfish arose at last to the surface again, he held some dirt in his claws. He had found some land deep in the water. Crawfish made a ball of the dirt and handed it to Chief Eagle, who then flew away with it. Four days later he returned to gather the birds. He announced to the council, "Now there is land, an island has been formed—follow me!"

The whole bird colony flew after Eagle to see the new land, though it was a very small island. Mysteriously, the land began to grow larger and larger as the water became lower and lower. More islands appeared and grew together, creating larger islands into one earth.

Strategy Review

1. Review "Cheerful Crawfish." Then, state a theme of the passage in your own words. Give a detail that supports the theme you stated.

_____

_____

_____

_____

_____

Strategy

Identify literary or structural elements and use them to understand the meaning of a text.

A *genre* is a type of literature, such as poetry, drama, or legend. If you can identify the genre of what you read, you can interpret what you read more easily.

2. How can you tell that "Cheerful Crawfish" is a legend or myth? Choose three answers.

(A) Animals talk and reason.

(B) Magical or unreal events happen.

(C) The story is set "before the beginning."

(D) The characters learn an important lesson.

(E) The story has a beginning, middle, and end.

Strategy

Reread texts to make comparisons, draw conclusions, or support inferences.

My hand is to me what your hearing and sight together are to you. In large measure we travel the same highways, read the same books, speak the same language, yet our experiences are different. All my comings and goings turn on the hand as on a pivot. It is the hand that binds me to the world of men and women. . . . With the dropping of a little word from another's hand into mine, a slight flutter of the fingers, began the intelligence, the joy, the fullness of my very life.

—Helen Keller, from *The World I Live In*

A childhood illness left Helen Keller deaf and blind, without the means to communicate with others. Her teacher, Annie Sullivan, helped her learn to communicate again by spelling words into her hand. Keller developed a deep love of language and became a writer, an adventurous outdoorswoman and avid boater, and a well-known American citizen around the world. She attended college with her teacher by her side, experienced art by touching art works, and even sensed music through the vibrations of instruments.

3. Part A: What can readers infer about Keller, based on her words and the passage?

(A) She did not care for art or music.

(B) She was not afraid to learn new things.

(C) She could communicate only through her teacher.

(D) She remained sad about losing her ability to see and hear.

Part B: Cite a detail from the excerpt that supports your answer to Part A.

_____

_____

_____

_____

Strategy Review

Strategy

Use word clues in a text to identify its structure, to see how ideas in a text are related, and to clarify word meanings.

Foley artists create the sound effects for television shows and for movies—the creaks, bangs, footsteps, slamming doors, and so on. Many people think that film sounds are simply recorded as the actors play the scenes. However, sets are not real places, and so the sounds made in sets don't sound real. For instance, a floor that looks like stone might really be painted wood, so footsteps on the floor sound like footsteps on wood. Foley artists replace the "wrong" footsteps with the "right" sound effect. Because sounds on film are usually a mix of recorded sounds, Foley artists experiment with combinations to give the world of film verity. That is, they make the world of film sound like viewers expect it to sound.

Transitions are words or phrases that show how ideas are connected. Words like *before*, *following*, or *next* can signal how events are related in time. Transitions like *because* or *so* can show a cause-effect relationship. Other transitions, such as *but* and *however*, signal contrast. Use the Internet to find lists of more transitions.

1. Write a phrase from the passage that tells readers an example is coming up.

_____

Context clues are words or phrases within a passage that help you understand unfamiliar words. Sometimes, the writer will make the definition obvious by using phrases that rename, describe, or give examples of the unfamiliar word. Look at the sentences before and after the unfamiliar word to find context clues.

2. Write the phrase from the passage that helps you find the meaning of the word *verity*.

_____

_____

_____

Strategy Review

Strategy | When writing, use details to support, explain, or clarify your main ideas.

[1] Biomimicry: the word combines *bio-*, meaning life, and *mimic*, meaning to imitate. [2] Engineers use biomimicry to build useful things based on nature. [3] Velcro, for example, is a very useful material. [4] It was inspired by tiny hooks on burrs. [5] I once had shoes that closed with Velcro rather than laces. [6] Chemists are studying lotus flower petals to understand how they stay perfectly clean even when growing in mud. [7] The chemists hope to develop paints that shed dirt, based on the design of the petals. [8] Nature offers inspiration for how to go fast, how to stay cold, and how to catch water. [9] These living, growing things are teaching people how to solve problems and meet needs.

Details can be either helpful or distracting. The writer of this passage knows that some readers will not know much about biomimicry. So, she provides several details to explain biomimicry. Examples, descriptions, and explanations of processes help, too. However, adding details that don't relate to the main idea may confuse readers.

1. **Which sentence in the passage presents a detail that does not relate to the main idea?**

   Ⓐ Sentence 1

   Ⓑ Sentence 3

   Ⓒ Sentence 5

   Ⓓ Sentence 8

When you have a writing assignment and not much time to plan, a scratch outline can help you quickly pull together ideas. These outlines get their name from the way they're written—very quickly and informally, maybe even scratched on a piece of scratch paper. A quick look at this outline shows that the writer has not gathered all the information needed for the opinion essay.

Scratch Outline for Opinion Essay

STEP 1: State your topic and your opinion about the topic.

My topic: *homework*

My opinion: *Students should have at least thirty minutes of homework each evening.*

Support for my opinion:	Objections to my opinion:
1. *There is not enough class time to practice skills.*	1. **Many students are involved in sports or music activities after school.**
2. *Reviewing skills soon after learning them helps students master them.*	2.
3.	3. **Students would rather play than do homework.**

Conclusion: *Thirty minutes of homework each evening is enough to help students review and retain what they learned during the school day.*

2. **Based on the outline, what does the writer need to do before drafting his opinion on homework requirements?**

   _____

   _____

   _____

   _____

   _____

   _____

Strategy Review

Strategy | Use transitions to show how ideas are related.

If you're going to go to the trouble to paint a room, do it right—the first time. To begin, clean the wall and trim carefully, and let it dry. _____, patch any little holes in the wall. You can get a patch kit at any home improvement store. Then, cover all furniture and carpets with drop cloths in case you spill paint. (You probably will spill a little). Gather your tools—brushes, rags, and rollers. Now you are ready, _____, to open the paint can and prepare to add a new color to your world.

When you need to describe a series of events, you can do so to tell readers how to do something, or you can do so to explain why things happen as they do. Use time transitions words such as *first*, *next*, and *finally* to show how events are related in time. Use cause-effect transitions such as *because* and *consequently* to show how causes and effects are related.

1. Write transitions that connect the steps in the painting process. Make sure each transition connects the ideas in a way that makes sense.

_____   _____

Strategy

Revise to make sure your writing is clear and makes sense. Then, edit to fix errors.

Writing is more interesting when it is clear. To make writing clear, think about how readers perceive the world. We use all our senses—sight, hearing, touch, taste, smell—to relate to the world. Even temperature and texture help us experience the world. Writers work to include sense details in their stories, to bring the stories to life. Here's how one writer described a storm approaching:

The smell of rain was in the heavy air, even though the thunder was still distant and muted. Sudden breezes gusted, scattering dry leaves this way and that and sending a message that the rain would soon arrive.

2. Write another sentence that includes sense details to describe how people might perceive the coming storm.

_____

_____

_____

3. Which of the following sentences contains incorrect punctuation?

Ⓐ Glancing at the darkening sky; Kate worried.

Ⓑ If the storm broke, the picnic would be ruined.

Ⓒ Thundered rumbled, but it was still far away.

Ⓓ The picnic was ready to serve: sandwiches, fruit, and bottles of water.

Strategies for Mathematics Tests

Read the strategies below to learn more about how they work.

Use rules, properties, or formulas to solve problems.
You can use rules, properties, and formulas to solve a variety of problems. For example, if you know the formula for the area of a rectangle, you can use a given length and width of the rectangle (or a rectangular garden) to quickly find its area. If you understand the commutative and distributive properties, you can rearrange an equation to solve it. If you understand the rules of the order of operations, you can correctly evaluate a mathematical expression.

Use drawings, graphs, or number lines to understand and solve a problem.
Many problems on a test can be modeled with a quick sketch, graph, or number line. These drawings can help you visualize the problem, figure out what you are being asked to find, or solve word problems.

Read word problems carefully to identify the given information and what you are being asked to find.
Whenever you encounter a word problem, you should first ask *What is the given information?* Then, you should ask *What question am I being asked to answer?* or *What am I being asked to find?* Don't start your calculations until you know the answers to these questions!

Look for key words in word problems that help you know which operation to use.
Key words in problems are signals that you should use certain operations. For example, the words *how much less* indicate subtraction. The words *total* and *altogether* often indicate addition. If you are asked to split something into equal portions, use division.

Organize and display data in order to interpret it.
Interpreting data means finding meaning in it. One way to find meaning in data is to organize it in a visual way. For example, dot plots are great for understanding data from a survey or poll. Line graphs show how two sets of data are related.

Apply prior knowledge and basic operations to solve problems.
Using what you already know about numbers and about the basic operations of addition, subtraction, multiplication, and division, you can solve problems involving decimals, fractions, geometry, and converting units of measurement. For example, you can use your understanding of division, multiplication, and place value to find area and to convert meters to centimeters.

Write and solve equations to solve real-world problems.
Translating everyday language into equations that use numbers, variables, and operations signs is an essential strategy. You will need to combine your understanding of several strategies to write and solve these equations, including understanding basic operations; applying rules, properties, and formulas; and looking for clues in the words to find needed information.

Math

Evaluate Numerical Expressions
Operations and Algebraic Thinking

DIRECTIONS: Choose or write the correct answer.

Strategy — When evaluating expressions, use the order of operations **PEMDAS**: **P**arentheses, **E**xponents, **M**ultiply or **D**ivide before **A**dd or **S**ubtract.

1. The expression below represents the number of students at Luisa's school who helped at the school fair. How many students helped at the school fair?

$$4 \times [33 - 3 \times (5 + 2)]$$

- (A) 840
- (B) 208
- (C) 80
- (D) 48

2. Which expressions have a value of 8? Choose all that apply.
- (A) $12 \times (4 + 2) \div 9$
- (B) $(4 \times 2) + (8 + 0) \div 8$
- (C) $36 \div 9 + [(4 \times 5) \div 5]$
- (D) $[5 (10 - 8) + 4] - 2 \times 3$
- (E) $(4 + 12 \div 3) + [12 - 3 \times (4 - 2)]$

3. Which two expressions have the same value as the expression below?

$$2\{10 \times [(33 + 25) - 25]\}$$

- (A) $10 \times (55 + 11) - 50 \times 2 + (200 \div 2)$
- (B) $\{[3 \times 20 + 5 \times 20 + 2{,}000 \div 2] - 10 \times 50\}$
- (C) $138 + \{550 - [6 + (25 - 10 \div 5)]\}$
- (D) $120 + (160 \times 4 \div 2) + 6 \times 20$
- (E) $\{120 + [2 + (400 - 200) \times 2] - 20$

4. Evaluate the expression $44 \times (9 + 3) \div 2$. Show your work.

5. Jake wrote the expression below to represent the number of minutes he practiced playing the guitar during the week. Evaluate the expression to show how long he practiced. Show your work.

$$5 \times 30 + 2 \times (30 + 15)$$

Evaluate Numerical Expressions
Operations and Algebraic Thinking

6. Mrs. Sanchez wrote this expression on the board for her students.

$$67 - 35 + 56 \div 2 - 6 + 4$$

Then, she realizes she wants 6 + 4 to be the first operation students perform when evaluating the expression. Write how this expression should look for the first operation to be 6 + 4. Explain your answer.

_____

_____

_____

Test Tip

Remember, there are 12 inches in one foot.

7. Jamal's height is 5 feet 9 inches. Write an expression that can be used to find Jamal's height in inches. Then, tell how many inches tall Jamal is.

8. Evaluate the expression 72 × (12 − 11) ÷ 8. Show your work.

9. Evaluate the following expression. Then, rewrite the expression so that it equals 11.

$$99 \div 11 - 2$$

_____

_____

10. Evaluate the following expression.

$$8 \times (21 - 6) \div (10 + 10)$$

Ⓐ 6
Ⓑ 26
Ⓒ 60
Ⓓ 260

11. Add parentheses to the following expression in two different ways to result in two different values. Show your work.

$$160 \div 20 \div 2 + 10$$

Write and Interpret Numerical Expressions
Operations and Algebraic Thinking

Strategy Identify word clues such as *first* and *then* to decide in which order to perform operations.

Test Tip Use word clues to create mathematical expressions from word problems.

1. Select the correct mathematical expression that represents *add 5 to 13 and then, multiply by 3.*

   (A) 5 + 13 x 3

   (B) 5 + (13 x 3)

   (C) (5 + 13) x 3

   (D) (5 x 13) + 3

2. For a school party, 15 students have each volunteered to bake a dozen muffins. Write an expression to represent the total number of muffins the students will bake.

   _____

3. Maudie saves $20 a week to buy a bike that costs $350. Maudie already has $260 when the bike is put on sale for $50 off. The sale lasts one month.

   Part A: Which information will NOT help you determine whether Maudie will have enough money to buy the bike for the lower price?

   (A) the sale price of the bike

   (B) how many weeks are in a month

   (C) how long Maudie has been saving

   (D) how much Maudie will save in one month

Part B: Choose the correct equation to determine whether Maudie will have enough to buy the bike for the lower price.

   (A) 260 + (4 x 20) = ?

   (B) 350 − 50 = ?

   (C) (260 ÷ 20) + (4 x 20) − (350 − 50) = ?

   (D) 260 + (4 x 20) − (350 − 50) = ?

Part C: Using the equation you selected, determine whether Maudie can buy the bike on sale. Show your work and explain your answer.

_____

_____

_____

_____

Write and Interpret Numerical Expressions
Operations and Algebraic Thinking

Strategy When comparing mathematical expressions, first identify terms that are the same. Then, identify how they are different.

4. Compare the following mathematical expressions and indicate whether each statement is true or false.

    A: 2 x (423 + 20,789)   B: 4 x (423 + 20,789)

    The value of A is two times
    the value of B.   true   false

    The value of B is two times
    the value of A.   true   false

    A + A = B   true   false

    B − A = A   true   false

    B + A = A + A   true   false

5. Compare the following mathematical expressions and choose the correct statement.

    A: (2 x 4) x (4 + 25)   B: (2 x 8) x (4 + 25)

    (A) The value of A is equal to the value of B.

    (B) The value of B is equal to the value of A.

    (C) The value of A is twice the value of B.

    (D) The value of A is half the value of B.

6. Three 6th grade classes are making flags for a school project. Each class will need 20 yards of blue fabric, 10 yards of red fabric, and 5 yards of yellow ribbon. If the amount of materials needed for one class is represented as 20b + 10r + 5y, choose all the expressions that represent the total amount of materials needed for all three classes.

    (A) 60b + 30r + 15y

    (B) (3 x 20b) + 10r + 5y

    (C) 3 x (20b + 10r + 5y)

    (D) 30b + 30r + 30y

7. Jessie is making bracelets for a fundraiser. Each bracelet will use 30 green beads, 6 black beads, and 12 silver beads. Write an expression that Jessie can use to find the total number of beads needed to make 25 bracelets. Then, find the amount of money Jessie will need to buy the beads if each bead costs $0.20. Show your work.

Use Numerical Patterns
Operations and Algebraic Thinking

Strategy | For patterns based on addition, use subtraction and work backward to check your work. For patterns based on multiplication, use division and work backward.

EXAMPLE
The table below shows an example of a numerical pattern based on the rule "Add 3" and using the starting number 0.

Add 3	0	3	6	9	12	15	18	21	24	27	30

1. Complete the following table using the rule "Add 5" and the rule "Add 10." The starting number for both tables is 0.

Add 5	0	5								
Add 10	0									

2. What is the rule for the pattern shown in the following table?

1	20	400	8,000	16,000	320,000

(A) Add 20

(B) Multiply by 2

(C) Multiply by 20

(D) Multiply by 200

3. Doug is planning a party. He has to plan where to seat people. He can seat one guest on each open end of a table. He must group the tables in rectangles. Look for a pattern and fill in the table.

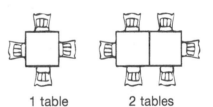

1 table   2 tables

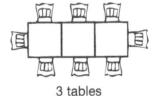 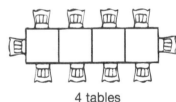

3 tables   4 tables

Number of Tables	1	2	3	4	5	6	7	8
Number of Guests	4	6	8	10				

4. Explain how the pattern grows.

_____

_____

5. If the pattern continues, how many guests will be able to sit at 10 tables?

_____

Graph Ordered Pairs
Operations and Algebraic Thinking

Strategy   Use a coordinate plane to graph ordered pairs of numbers. Use your graph to answer questions.

Test Tip   A plane must travel along the ground before it takes off. So, when graphing, move left to right along the *x*-axis first; then, move up or down.

1. Complete the following table using the rule "Add 2" and the rule "Add 4."

Add 2	0	2			8	10
Add 4	0	4	8			20

Form ordered pairs from the two patterns.

(0, 0) (2, 4) (4, _____) (_____, _____)

(8, _____) (10, 20)

Graph the ordered pairs

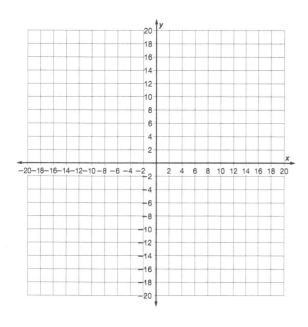

2. The following table uses the rule "Add 1" and the rule "Add 2." The starting number for both tables is 0.

Add 1	0	1	2	3	4	5	6	7	8	9	10
Add 2	0	2	4	6	8	10	12	14	16	18	20

Form ordered pairs from the two patterns.

_____

_____

Describe the relationship between the paired numbers.

_____

_____

Graph the ordered pairs.

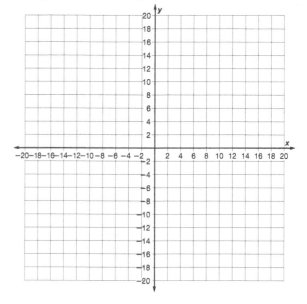

Math

Place Value Patterns
Numbers and Operations

Strategy — Use place value to write numbers in expanded notation. Write each digit multiplied by its place value. Start with the largest place value.

Test Tip — The place value of each digit is 10 times the place value of the digit to its right.

EXAMPLE
Write the number in expanded notation.
56,456
(5 x 10,000) + (6 x 1,000) + (4 x 100) + (5 x 10) + (6 x 1)

1. Write each number in expanded notation.

322

_____

257,982

_____

2. For the following number, complete the table by writing the digit in the box next to the appropriate place value.

6,875

Place Value	Digit
1,000	
100	
10	
1	

3. The following number is written in expanded notation. Write the number in standard notation.

(8 x 1,000,000) + (8 x 100,000) + (8 x 10,000) + (6 x 1,000) + (8 x 100) + (9 x 10) + (8 x 1)

(A) 8,668,898

(B) 8,686,898

(C) 8,866,898

(D) 8,886,898

4. Write the number shown in expanded notation in standard notation.

(3 x 100) + (0 x 10) + (2 x 1)

_____

5. Write the number shown in standard notation in expanded notation.

900,009

_____

Place Value Patterns
Numbers and Operations

Strategy Create a table to use place value in multi-digit numbers. Write each digit in its correct place value: thousandths, hundreds, tens, ones.

Test Tip In a multi-digit number, the place value of each digit is $\frac{1}{10}$ times the place value of the digit to its left.

EXAMPLE
The following number is written in expanded notation.
$(4 \times \frac{1}{10}) + (5 \times \frac{1}{100}) + (6 \times \frac{1}{1000})$
This is the same number written in standard notation: 0.456

6. The following number is written in expanded notation.

$(3 \times 10) + (2 \times 1) + (2 \times \frac{1}{10}) + (3 \times \frac{1}{100})$

Which number in standard notation is equivalent?

(A) 232.3

(B) 322.3

(C) 32.23

(D) 23.23

7. The following number is written in standard notation. Write the number in expanded form.

0.45

_____

8. The following number is written in expanded notation.

$(7 \times \frac{1}{10}) + (9 \times \frac{1}{100}) + (9 \times \frac{1}{1000})$

Which number in standard notation is equivalent?

(A) 0.0799

(B) 0.799

(C) 7.99

(D) 79.9

9. The following number is written in expanded notation.

$(8 \times 1000) + (7 \times 100) + (2 \times 10) + (9 \times 1) +$
$(5 \times \frac{1}{10}) + (5 \times \frac{1}{100})$

Write the number in standard notation.

_____

Powers of 10
Numbers and Operations

Strategy — Use exponents to convert the power of 10 to standard notation. Then, use the standard notation number in your calculations.

Test Tip — Read all parts of the question first.

1. The following numbers are expressed as multiples of powers of 10. Write the numbers as whole numbers in standard notation.

$$(6 \times 10^1) = (6 \times 10) =$$

_____

$$(8 \times 10^3) = (8 \times 1,000) =$$

_____

2. The table below shows powers of 10 for whole numbers.

10^0	10^1	10^2	10^3	10^4	10^5
1	10	100	1,000	10,000	100,000

Complete the table below for additional powers of 10.

		10^8	10^9
1,000,000	10,000,000		

Test Tip

When multiplying by powers of 10, use this pattern to check your work and make sure your answer has the correct number of digits.

3. Explain the relationship between the power of 10 and the number of zeroes in the corresponding number. Give an example.

_____

_____

_____

4. Write the following numbers as multiples of powers of 10.

90,000

_____

4

_____

700

_____

5. The following number is expressed in expanded notation. Write the number as multiples of powers of 10 and in standard notation.

$$(3 \times 1000) + (2 \times 100) + (6 \times 10)$$

_____

_____

Powers of 10
Numbers and Operations

DIRECTIONS: Multiply or divide by powers of 10. Write the answers as whole numbers or decimals.

> **Strategy**
>
> Check your work by reading it in words.
> For example, $25 \div 1{,}000 = 0.025$ can be read as "twenty-five divided by one thousand equals twenty-five thousandths."

6. $9 \div 10^0 = 9 \div 1 =$ _____

7. $20 \div 10^3 = 20 \div 1{,}000 =$ _____

8. $0.5 \times$ _____ $= 5$

9. $6 \div$ _____ $= 0.06$

10. $9 \div$ _____ $= 0.009$

11. $0.6 \times$ _____ $= 6{,}000$

12. **Part A: Dani and Marcus are measuring distances in the lab. They record some of the distances in centimeters and others in meters. They know that 1 meter = 100 centimeters, so they decide to use powers of 10 to convert all their measurements to meters so they can compare distances. Their results are shown in the table below.**

Measurement in centimeters (A)	Measurement in meters (B)
45	0.45
203	2.03
97	0.97
3.5	0.035

What is the correct equation for converting centimeters to meters?

Ⓐ $A \times 10^2 = B$

Ⓑ $A \div 10^2 = B$

Ⓒ $A \times 10^3 = B$

Ⓓ $A \div 10^3 = B$

Part B: Dani and Marcus begin to notice a pattern and realize they can convert their measurements without performing a calculation each time. Choose all that describe the pattern they discover.

Ⓐ To convert centimeters to meters, move the decimal point two spaces to the right.

Ⓑ To convert meters to centimeters, move the decimal point two spaces to the right.

Ⓒ To convert centimeters to meters, move the decimal point two spaces to the left.

Ⓓ To convert meters to centimeters, move the decimal point two spaces to the left.

Read and Write Decimals
Numbers and Operations

Strategy | Use place value to the right of the decimal point to write decimals in expanded form.

1. Write the following numbers in expanded form.

5.642

2. 4,257.21

3. Choose all the equations that are true.

(A) 22,336.462 = (2 × 10,000) + (2 × 1,000) +

(3 × 100) + (3 × 10) + (6 × 1) + (4 × $\frac{1}{10}$ +

(6 × $\frac{1}{100}$) + (2 × $\frac{1}{1000}$)

(B) 0.846 = (8 × $\frac{1}{100}$) + (4 × $\frac{1}{1000}$) + (6 × $\frac{1}{10,000}$)

(C) 3,047.45 = (3 × 1,000) + (4 × 10) + (7 × 1) +

(4 × $\frac{1}{10}$) + (5 × $\frac{1}{100}$)

(D) 6.006 = (6 × 1) + (6 × $\frac{1}{1000}$)

Strategy

When writing numbers in expanded form, start by determining how many terms your answer will have; you should have as many terms as there are digits in the number.

4. Write 2.25 in word form.

_____

5. Choose the number that is equivalent to *three thousand forty-five and seven thousandths.*

(A) 3,045.007

(B) 3,450.007

(C) 3,450.007

(D) 3,045.07

6. Write 75,296.999 in word form.

_____

_____

_____

_____

7. Write 3.75 in word form.

_____

8. Choose the number that is equivalent to *two thousand fifty-five and six thousandths.*

(A) 2,550.06

(B) 2,055.006

(C) 2,650.006

(D) 2,056.06

Compare Decimals
Numbers and Operations

Strategy   Use numbers and place value to compare pairs of decimals.

Test Tip   Remember that < is read "less than" and > is read "greater than."

1. **For each pair of numbers below, use >, =, or < to show whether the first number (A) is greater than, equal to, or less than the second number (B).**

A	>, =, <	B
52.16		52.17
30.99		30.990
200.02		200.002
0.123		0.223

2. **For each pair of numbers below, use >, =, or < to show whether the first number (A) is greater than, equal to, or less than the second number (B).**

A	>, =, <	B
99.50		99.5000
154.120		154.089
5,789.2		57,892.8
0.094		0.0094

3. **Order the following numbers from greatest to least by writing a 1, 2, 3, or 4 in the boxes below.**

☐ $(6 \times \frac{1}{100})$

☐ (2.2×1000)

☐ $(2 \times \frac{1}{1000})$

☐ (12×1000)

4. **Jessie buys two pieces of candy. One weighs one tenth of a pound and the other weighs 94 thousandths of a pound. Jessie tells her brother he can have the larger piece and offers him the first piece. He says the second piece is larger because 94 is greater than 1 and 1000 is greater than 10.**

Who is right, Jessie or her brother?

_____

Explain how you know which piece is larger.

_____

_____

_____

_____

_____

_____

Round Decimals
Numbers and Operations

DIRECTIONS: Read each question. Choose or write the correct answer.

> **Strategy** — Use place value to round decimals. Look at the digit following the place value you are rounding to. If the digit is 5 or higher, round up.

1. Round 536.28 to the nearest tenth.

   (A) 536

   (B) 536.2

   (C) 536.3

   (D) 536.29

> **Test Tip**
>
> Think of a number line. Ask yourself, *What two numbers is this number between? Which number is it closer to?*

2. Round 100.92 to the nearest whole number.

   (A) 100

   (B) 101

   (C) 100.9

   (D) 100.93

3. Round 57.2 to the nearest 10.

   (A) 50

   (B) 57

   (C) 58

   (D) 60

4. Round 47.65 to the nearest tenth.

   _____

5. Round 850.049 to the nearest 100.

   _____

6. Round 0.075 to the nearest hundredth.

   _____

7. Round 1,286.007 to the nearest hundredth.

   (A) 1,286

   (B) 1,286.1

   (C) 1,286.01

   (D) 1,286.107

8. Janice is asked to round 0.604 to the nearest whole number on a test. She says the correct answer is 1. Is she correct? If she made a mistake, explain her mistake.

   _____

   _____

9. Barry is asked to round 30.217 to the nearest 10 on a homework assignment. He says the correct answer is 30.22. Is he correct? If he made a mistake, explain his mistake.

   _____

   _____

   _____

   _____

Round Decimals
Numbers and Operations

Strategy Approach problems with dollars and cents as any other decimal. Rounding money is the same as rounding any decimal. Remember to add a dollar sign to your answer.

10. Anna saved $35.72 from her babysitting jobs. How much does Anna have, rounded to the nearest dollar?

   (A) $35.00
   (B) $36.00
   (C) $35.70
   (D) $35.80

11. Henry found $2.63 in change around the house. He already has $5.49 in his piggy bank. How much money does Henry have, rounded to the nearest dime?

   _____

   Write how you found your answer.

   _____

   _____

12. Arianna has $15.42. Gavin has $27.33. If they combine their money, how much will they have to the nearest dollar?

   _____

13. Sam found $3.65 at the playground. He already has $4.77 saved. How much money does Sam have, rounded to the nearest dime?

   _____

14. Jennifer spent $26.83 at the store. How much did Jennifer spend, rounded to the nearest dollar?

   (A) $26.00
   (B) $26.80
   (C) $26.30
   (D) $27.00

15. Andrew got $20.00 for his birthday. He bought a video game that cost $11.94. How much money does Andrew have left, rounded to the nearest dime?

   (A) $31.90
   (B) $8.10
   (C) $8.06
   (D) $8.00

16. Ellie is training for a half-marathon. She ran:

   • 7.2 miles on Monday
   • 3.75 miles on Tuesday
   • 12.875 miles on Wednesday
   • 5.126 miles on Thursday
   • 11.7 miles on Friday

   How many miles did Ella run during the week, rounded to the nearest hundredth of a mile?

   _____

Multiply and Divide
Number and Operations

DIRECTIONS: Solve each problem. Show your work.

Strategy Use basic math facts to multiply and divide multi-digit numbers.

Test Tip Pay attention to place value when you calculate. Estimate your answer to make sure it is reasonable.

1. $492 \times 38 =$

4. $1,525 \times 35 =$

2. $463 \times 825 =$

(A) 33,335
(B) 33,375
(C) 53,335
(D) 53,375

5. There are 52 weeks in each year, and Salih walks his dog 14 times each week. How many times does Salih walk his dog each year?

3. $305 \times 51 =$

(A) 15,551
(B) 15,555
(C) 150,551
(D) 150,555

Multiply and Divide
Numbers and Operations

DIRECTIONS: Solve each problem. Show your work.

Strategy | Identify clue words or operations symbols in word problems to know whether to multiply or divide.

6. $1,728 \div 24 =$

9. $4,640 \div 32 =$

7. $777 \div 7 =$

Ⓐ 140
Ⓑ 145
Ⓒ 150
Ⓓ 155

10. **Martine solved the following division problem: 549 ÷ 9 = 61. Write an equation she could use to estimate and see if her answer is reasonable.**

_____

_____

8. $2,185 \div 5 =$

11. **Nathan checked his work on a problem by estimating using the following equation: 900 ÷ 10 = 90. Write an equation he could have been checking. Give the exact answer to your equation.**

_____

_____

Ⓐ 437
Ⓑ 447
Ⓒ 537
Ⓓ 547

Add and Subtract Decimals
Numbers and Operations

DIRECTIONS: Solve each problem.

Strategy   Use adding and subtracting whole numbers to add and subtract decimals.

Test Tip   Look carefully at the equation to know which operation to perform. Remember to line up the decimal points.

1. $2.14 + 3.01 =$ _____

2. $18.7 - 12.05 =$ _____

3. Natalie wrote that $773.15 - 200.4 = 2,531$. What mistake did she make?

_____

_____

4. $664.72 + 323.85 =$
   (A) 988.57
   (B) 340.87
   (C) 987.157
   (D) 9.8857

5. Chris bought a phone for $250.63. He paid $35.15 for a case. What was the total amount he spent?

_____

6. $1.37 - 0.52 =$ _____

7. Cameron bought a CD for $15.45. He paid $1.16 in tax. What was the total cost of the CD?

_____

8. Julia bought a pair of boots for $45.50. She had a coupon for $10 off and paid $1.78 in sales tax. What was the total cost of the boots? Show your work.

9. Mallory bought a bag of cat food for $15.41. She had a coupon for $5.00 off and paid $1.08 in sales tax. How much did she spend all together? Show your work.

Add and Subtract Decimals
Numbers and Operations

DIRECTIONS: Solve each problem.

Strategy Treat word problems with money as whole numbers and decimals.

10. Rogan ordered a sandwich for $5.95 and a glass of milk for $1.50. He paid $0.75 in tax and left a tip of $1.75. What was the total cost of the meal? Show your work.

DIRECTIONS: Write a statement telling whether each answer is correct or incorrect. If an answer is incorrect, tell what the correct answer is.

14. $142.76 + 86.2 = 156.38$

_____

_____

15. $30.83 - 7.99 = 37.16$

_____

_____

11. $804.16 - 155.3 =$
   - (A) 788.63
   - (B) 959.46
   - (C) 648.86
   - (D) 648.13

16. $251.39 - 207.8 = 43.59$

_____

_____

12. $25.34 + 16.08 =$ _____

13. $363.51 - $48.63 =$
   - (A) $304.88
   - (B) $412.14
   - (C) $314.80
   - (D) $314.88

17. $303.03 + 606.09 = 909.02$

_____

_____

18. $60.82 - 41.63 = 19.19$

_____

_____

Multiply and Divide Decimals
Numbers and Operations

DIRECTIONS: Solve each problem. Show your work.

Strategy | Use adding and subtracting whole numbers to multiply and divide decimals.

1. $27.4 \times 8.1 =$

4. $103.8 \div 3 =$

(A) 22,194
(B) 221.94
(C) 2,219.4
(D) 22.194

(A) 3.46
(B) 346
(C) 34.6
(D) 415.2

2. $35.2 \div 4 =$ _____

5. $225.25 \div 5 =$

Test Tip

When you are dividing, don't forget to place the decimal point in the quotient directly above the decimal point in the dividend.

(A) 450.5
(B) 4.505
(C) 4,505
(D) 45.05

6. $19.7 \times 10.5 =$ _____

3. $7.63 \times 2.11 =$ _____

Multiply and Divide Decimals
Numbers and Operations

DIRECTIONS: Read each story problem carefully. Then, choose or write the best answer.

Strategy Draw a model to help you solve the problem.

7. Eli would like to run a marathon, which is 26.2 miles. His goal is to finish it in 6 hours. What is the average speed Eli has to run to meet his goal? Round your answer to the nearest hundredth.

_____

8. Lillian earns 8.25 per hour. If she works 37.75 hours in a week, how much will she earn? Round your answer to the nearest cent.

_____

9. It is 457.2 miles from Max's house to his grandmother's house. If his father drives 55 miles per hour the entire way, how long will it take to get there? Round your answer to the nearest hundredth.

_____

10. Tyler walks 2.31 miles a day for 7 days. How many miles total does he walk? Round your answer to the nearest hundredth.

_____

11. The price of a day pass at the public pool is $6.75 per person. There are 5 people in Evelyn's family. How much will it cost for the entire family to go to the pool for the day? Round your answer to the nearest cent.

_____

12. The area of Isaac's kitchen is 187.5 square feet. The kitchen is 15 feet long. What is the width of the kitchen?
   (A) 22.5 m
   (B) 22.5 ft
   (C) 12.5 m
   (D) 12.5 ft

13. Bailey sells pizzas for $12.18 each. If he sells 16 pizzas, how much will he make? Round your answer to the nearest cent.

_____

Fractions with Unlike Denominators
Numbers and Operations

DIRECTIONS: Solve each problem. All answers should be in lowest terms.

Strategy   Use what you know about common multiples to find the least common denominator of the two fractions. Then, add or subtract.

Test Tip   A common denominator will be a multiple of both denominators.

EXAMPLE:

$$\frac{1}{11} + \frac{1}{33} = \frac{4}{33}$$

1. $\frac{3}{5} - \frac{1}{2} =$

   (A) $\frac{4}{7}$

   (B) $\frac{2}{3}$

   (C) $\frac{1}{10}$

   (D) $\frac{2}{10}$

2. $\frac{4}{7} + \frac{2}{3} =$ _____ = _____

3. $\frac{3}{4} - \frac{2}{3} =$

   (A) $\frac{1}{1}$

   (B) 1

   (C) $\frac{1}{12}$

   (D) $\frac{9}{8}$

4. $\frac{4}{3} + \frac{5}{9} =$ _____ = _____

5. $\frac{1}{2} - \frac{2}{8} =$

   (A) $\frac{2}{8}$

   (B) $\frac{1}{4}$

   (C) $\frac{1}{6}$

   (D) $\frac{3}{4}$

6. $\frac{15}{18} - \frac{4}{9} =$ _____

7. $\frac{8}{12} + \frac{1}{3} =$ _____

8. $\frac{3}{7} - \frac{4}{14} =$ _____

Fractions with Unlike Denominators
Numbers and Operations

DIRECTIONS: Solve each problem. Show your work, and write your answers in lowest terms.

Strategy Read the problem carefully. Draw fraction models to help you answer the questions.

EXAMPLE:

Elizabeth ate $\frac{1}{3}$ of the pizza. Lyla ate $\frac{2}{5}$ of the pizza. How much more pizza did Lyla eat?

Answer: $\frac{1}{15}$ more

9. Johnny rode his bicycle $\frac{4}{5}$ mile one day and $\frac{2}{3}$ mile the next. How far did Johnny ride his bicycle those two days? Show your work.

10. During a class party, $\frac{2}{3}$ of a cheese pizza and $\frac{4}{6}$ of a pepperoni pizza were eaten. How much pizza was eaten all together? Show your work.

11. Nathan bought $\frac{1}{2}$ pound of raisins. On the way home, he ate $\frac{1}{4}$ of a pound. How many pounds of raisins did Nathan have when he got home? Show your work.

12. In a mile relay race, Emma ran $\frac{3}{5}$ of a mile and Lori ran the rest. What fraction of a mile did Lori run?

(A) $\frac{1}{5}$

(B) $\frac{2}{5}$

(C) $\frac{1}{6}$

(D) $\frac{2}{6}$

Explore Division
Numbers and Operations

DIRECTIONS: Read each problem. Then, choose or write the best answer.

> **Strategy** Use division to solve each problem. Write an equation or use picture models to find your answer.

1. Mrs. Rios ordered pizza for her class of 30 students. The pizza is cut into 45 pieces. How many slices of pizza can each student have?

   _____

   Write how you found your answer.

   _____

   _____

2. Samuel has to read a book that is 75 pages long. He has 4 days in which to read it. If he reads the same number of pages each day, how many pages must Samuel read per day to get his assignment done?

   (A) $18\frac{1}{2}$

   (B) 18

   (C) $18\frac{3}{4}$

   (D) 19

> **Strategy**
> Remember to make your remainder into a fraction and then, reduce to lowest terms.

3. Lucy's mother bought a 50-pound bag of rice at the store. She wants to share it evenly with her three sisters. How much rice will each sister get?

   (A) 12 pounds

   (B) $12\frac{1}{2}$ pounds

   (C) 13 pounds

   (D) 10 pounds with 10 pounds left over

4. Grayson has 37 baseball cards. He wants to put them in an album with 5 cards on each page. Which equation would Grayson use to figure out how many pages he will need?

   (A) $5 \div 37 =$

   (B) $37 \times 5 =$

   (C) $37 + 5 =$

   (D) $37 \div 5 =$

5. Mrs. Jessup bought 128 ounces of juice for her son's birthday party. There are 8 children at the party. Will she have enough juice to give each child 2 8-ounce cups of juice?

   _____

   Write how you found your answer.

   _____

   _____

   _____

   _____

Explore Division
Numbers and Operations

Strategy	When things are split into equal groups, always use division.

6. The Sanders family is taking a road trip. They are planning to travel 274 miles in 3 days. If they drive the same number of miles each day, how many miles will they have to drive each day?

_____

Write how you found your answer.

_____

_____

_____

_____

7. Claire has 11 sticks of gum. She wants to share it with her 2 sisters. How many sticks of gum will each girl get?

Ⓐ 3

Ⓑ 4

Ⓒ $3\frac{1}{2}$

Ⓓ $3\frac{2}{3}$

8. Tyler and Zachary earned $53 mowing lawns. They want to split the money evenly. Which equation should they use to find out how much money each should get?

Ⓐ $53 \div 2 =$

Ⓑ $53 \times 2 =$

Ⓒ $2 \div 53 =$

Ⓓ $2 \times 53 =$

How much money should each boy get?

_____

9. The report that Makayla has to write for social studies must be 5 pages long. She has 4 hours to type it. How many pages must she type each hour to finish on time?

_____

10. Kylie biked at a steady pace for 2 hours. She rode 15 miles. How fast did Kylie ride?

Ⓐ 7 miles per hour

Ⓑ 15 miles per hour

Ⓒ $7\frac{1}{2}$ miles per hour

Ⓓ $8\frac{1}{4}$ miles per hour

11. Write a story problem to match the equation $35 \div 4 = 8\frac{3}{4}$.

_____

_____

_____

_____

_____

_____

Multiply Fractions
Numbers and Operations

DIRECTIONS: Read each problem. Then, choose or write the best answer.

Strategy Use multiplication rules to multiply whole numbers and fractions.

Test Tip Think of a whole number as a fraction with a denominator of 1.

1. A batch of cookies calls for $\frac{3}{4}$ cup of sugar. Audrey wants to make 4 times as many cookies as the recipe makes. How much sugar does she need?

   Ⓐ $\frac{9}{4} = 2\frac{1}{4}$ cups

   Ⓑ $\frac{19}{4} = 4\frac{3}{4}$ cups

   Ⓒ $\frac{12}{4} = 3$ cups

   Ⓓ $\frac{7}{4} = 1\frac{3}{4}$ cups

2. Wyatt and his friends ate $\frac{3}{4}$ of the bagels in the bag. There were a dozen bagels. Draw a model to show how many bagels the boys ate.

3. Charlie gets $28 a week in allowance. He puts $\frac{1}{2}$ of the money in savings, uses $\frac{1}{4}$ to pay for his piano lesson, and spends the last $\frac{1}{4}$ on snacks. How much does Charlie pay for piano lessons?

   _____

   Write how you found your answer.

   _____

   _____

Test Tip

Read the question carefully to make sure you are answering the right question.

4. Hunter made 36 colored eggs. He colored $\frac{1}{3}$ of them purple, $\frac{1}{3}$ of them green, and $\frac{1}{3}$ of them yellow. How many purple eggs did Hunter have?

   Ⓐ 12

   Ⓑ $\frac{1}{3}$

   Ⓒ 8

   Ⓓ $\frac{2}{3}$

5. Gabriella picked $\frac{3}{4}$ of a pound of strawberries. That afternoon, she ate $\frac{1}{2}$ of the strawberries. How many pounds of strawberries were left?

   _____

   Write how you found your answer.

   _____

   _____

6. David helped his mother bake cookies. They used $\frac{2}{3}$ of a cup of nuts for chocolate chip cookies. They used twice as many nuts for peanut butter cookies. How many cups of nuts did they use in the peanut butter cookies?

   Ⓐ $\frac{2}{3}$

   Ⓑ $1\frac{2}{3}$

   Ⓒ $1\frac{1}{3}$

   Ⓓ 1

Find Area
Numbers and Operations

DIRECTIONS: Read each problem. Then, choose or write the best answer.

Strategy   Use the formula for finding area and the rules for multiplying fractions to find the areas of rectangles.

1. Find the area of the rectangle.

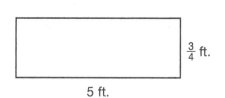

5 ft.

Test Tip

Remember, to find area, multiply length by width.

2. Find the area of the rectangle.

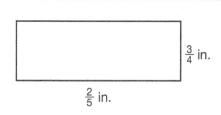

Write how you found your answer.

_____

_____

3. Jackson Park is shaped like a rectangle. Use the drawing to find the area of the park.

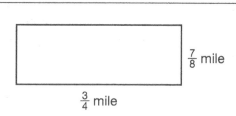

4. Maya made a model of her bedroom. The floor is a rectangle with a length of 3 inches and a width of $\frac{7}{8}$ inch. What is the area of the floor in Maya's model?

Ⓐ $3\frac{7}{8}$ square inches

Ⓑ $2\frac{5}{8}$ square inches

Ⓒ $\frac{7}{24}$ square inches

Ⓓ $\frac{37}{8}$ square inches

Understand Scaling
Numbers and Operations

DIRECTIONS: Read each problem. Then, choose or write the best answer.

Strategy   Use multiplication rules to understand scaling.

1. A blueprint has a scale of 1 inch : 5 feet. A wall in the blueprint is $3\frac{1}{2}$ inches long. How long should the actual wall be?

   Ⓐ 25 feet

   Ⓑ $17\frac{1}{2}$ feet

   Ⓒ 15 feet

   Ⓓ $15\frac{1}{2}$ feet

Write the equation you used to solve this problem.

_____

Test Tip

Before you choose an answer, ask yourself if the answer makes sense. If you are confused by a problem, read it again. If you are still confused, skip the problem and come back to it later.

2. A model car has a scale of 1 cm : 10 inches. The radius of the model car's wheel is $1\frac{1}{2}$ cm. What equation would you use to find the radius of the actual car?

_____

3. Allison is copying a picture for her art class. But, she is multiplying each measure of the original picture by $1\frac{1}{2}$. Will Allison's copy of the picture be larger than, smaller than, or the same size as the original picture?

Write how you know.

_____

_____

4. Sebastian is baking a batch of cookies for the bake sale. He multiplied the measure of each ingredient by $\frac{1}{2}$. Is the batch of cookies going to be larger than, smaller than, or the same size as the batch made in the original recipe?

_____

Write how you know.

_____

_____

5. Which value is greater: 53 or $\frac{3}{4} \times 53$?

_____

6. Which value is greater: 72 or $1\frac{1}{3} \times 72$?

_____

7. Which value is greater: $\frac{5}{6} \times 12$ or $\frac{6}{6} \times 12$?

_____

Write how you know.

_____

_____

_____

_____

Understand Scaling
Numbers and Operations

Strategy Use a scale factor to reduce or enlarge a number.

Test Tip A scale factor is a number that is multiplied by another number to shrink or enlarge something.

8. Cooper used plans from the Internet to build a clubhouse. The plans show the front of the clubhouse as 2 inches long. The front of Cooper's clubhouse is 8 feet long. What was the scale on the plans?

(A) 1 in. : 3 ft.

(B) 2 in. : 2 ft.

(C) 1 in. : 4 ft.

(D) 1 in. : 8 ft.

9. Which answer shows a scale that would double the size of an object?

(A) $1 : \frac{1}{2}$

(B) $2 : 1$

(C) $2 : \frac{1}{2}$

(D) $1 : 2$

10. Write a multiplication problem that would enlarge a 3-inch object by $\frac{1}{3}$.

_____

11. Write a multiplication problem that would shrink a 5-foot object by $\frac{1}{2}$.

_____

12. Elena is having a dinner party for herself and 7 guests. She found a recipe that serves 4. What should she do to each ingredient to scale the recipe for her party?

(A) multiply each measure by 8

(B) multiply each measure by $\frac{1}{8}$

(C) multiply each measure by 2

(D) multiply each measure by $\frac{1}{2}$

13. Stella reduced a recipe from serving 12 to serving 4. What did she do to each ingredient in the recipe?

(A) multiplied by $\frac{1}{3}$

(B) multiplied by 3

(C) multiplied by 4

(D) multiplied by $\frac{1}{4}$

14. A square has a side length of 4 inches. If you enlarge the square by a scale of 4, what will the area of the new square be?

(A) 16 square inches

(B) 256 square inches

(C) 64 square inches

(D) 32 square inches

Write how you found your answer.

_____

_____

Multiply Fractions and Mixed Numbers
Numbers and Operations

DIRECTIONS: Read each problem. Then, choose or write the best answer.

Strategy Use rules for multiplying fractions and improper fractions to multiply mixed numbers.

Test Tip Change mixed numbers to improper fractions before multiplying.

1. David caught a $7\frac{1}{2}$ pound fish. His brother caught a fish that was $\frac{1}{4}$ as big. How much did his brother's fish weigh?

   (A) $1\frac{7}{8}$ pounds

   (B) $7\frac{1}{4}$ pounds

   (C) $1\frac{3}{4}$ pounds

   (D) 7 pounds

2. Annabelle made $2\frac{1}{2}$ cups of rice. She ate $\frac{3}{4}$ of it at dinner. How much rice does she have left over?

   (A) $1\frac{3}{4}$ cups

   (B) $1\frac{7}{8}$ cups

   (C) 2 cups

   (D) $1\frac{1}{2}$ cups

3. It is $2\frac{1}{4}$ miles to school. Anthony walks every day. How many miles does Anthony walk each week?

   _____

   Write how you found your answer.

   _____

   _____

   _____

   _____

4. A bag of dog food weighs $12\frac{1}{2}$ pounds. How many pounds of dog food are left when the bag is $\frac{3}{4}$ empty?

   (A) $9\frac{3}{8}$ pounds

   (B) $3\frac{1}{8}$ pounds

   (C) $8\frac{1}{4}$ pounds

   (D) $3\frac{1}{2}$ pounds

   Write how you found your answer.

   _____

   _____

5. Savannah has 26 snow globes in her collection. Nora has $1\frac{1}{2}$ times as many bells in her collection. How many bells does Nora have in her collection?

   (A) 39

   (B) 13

   (C) $24\frac{1}{2}$

   (D) $27\frac{1}{2}$

Multiply Fractions and Mixed Numbers
Numbers and Operations

Strategy   Use models or equations to solve the problem.

Test Tip   Use estimation to check if your answer makes sense.

6. Christian is $2\frac{1}{2}$ times as old as Colton. Colton is 7. How old is Christian?

_____

7. What is the area of an $8\frac{1}{2}$ by 11-inch sheet of paper?

_____

8. Reagan went to see a movie that was $2\frac{1}{2}$ hours long. Her friend Scarlett saw another movie that was $\frac{3}{4}$ as long. How long was the movie Scarlett saw?

(A) $3\frac{1}{4}$ hours

(B) $1\frac{3}{4}$ hours

(C) $1\frac{7}{8}$ hours

(D) 2 hours

9. Dominic's front yard is a rectangle. It is $15\frac{1}{2}$ feet long and $10\frac{2}{3}$ feet wide. What is the area of Dominic's front yard?

_____

10. Samantha ran $2\frac{6}{7}$ miles. Austin ran $2\frac{2}{3}$ times as far. How far did Austin run?

_____

11. Miss Clark wants to buy fabric to cover her bulletin board. The board is $4\frac{1}{2}$ feet long and 6 feet wide. What is the area that Miss Clark has to cover?

(A) $10\frac{1}{2}$ square feet

(B) $24\frac{1}{2}$ square feet

(C) $27\frac{1}{4}$ square feet

(D) 27 square feet

12. John is making a model of a pack of gum. The pack is $2\frac{2}{3}$ inches long. He wants to make the model $2\frac{1}{2}$ times as big as the real thing. How long should he make the model?

(A) $4\frac{3}{5}$ inches

(B) $4\frac{1}{3}$ inches

(C) $6\frac{2}{3}$ inches

(D) $2\frac{1}{2}$ inches

Divide with Fractions
Numbers and Operations

DIRECTIONS: Read each problem. Then, choose or write the best answer.

Strategy | Use division to divide quantities into equal groups or portions.

Test Tip | Read each question carefully to decide if you are dividing a whole number by a fraction or a fraction by a whole number.

1. Parker and Isaiah have $\frac{1}{2}$ of a bag of popcorn. They want to split it evenly. What fraction of a bag of popcorn will each boy get? Draw a picture or write an equation in the box to solve the problem.

2. Mrs. Yablako has 5 apples. If she divides each apple in half, how many children can have a piece of apple for snack? Draw a picture or write an equation in the box to solve the problem.

Strategy

Make a sketch to help you solve the problems.

3. Levi bought a $\frac{1}{3}$ pound bag of chips for the class party. He wants to split it evenly into 3 bowls. Which picture shows how much will be in each bowl?

 Ⓐ    Ⓑ

 Ⓒ    Ⓓ

How much will be in each bowl?

_____

4. Stella's parents bought her a $\frac{1}{4}$ pound box of chocolates for her birthday. She eats an equal amount each day for 4 days until the candy is gone. Which equation shows how much candy Stella eats each day?

Ⓐ $4 \div \frac{1}{4} = 16$ pounds

Ⓑ $4 \times \frac{1}{4} = 1$ pound

Ⓒ $\frac{1}{4} \div 4 = \frac{1}{16}$ pound

Ⓓ $\frac{1}{4} - \frac{1}{4} = 0$ pounds

5. Mrs. Torte baked 3 cakes. Which equation shows how many pieces of cake she will have if she divides each cake into 16 equal parts?

Ⓐ $3 \times \frac{1}{16} = \frac{3}{16}$

Ⓑ $3 \div \frac{1}{16} = 48$

Ⓒ $3 + \frac{1}{16} = 3\frac{1}{16}$

Ⓓ $\frac{1}{16} \div 3 = \frac{3}{16}$

Divide with Fractions
Numbers and Operations

DIRECTIONS: Choose or write the expression that proves the answer is correct.

> **Strategy** To check a division answer, multiply the quotient by the divisor. If you get the dividend, then your answer is correct. Don't forget to simplify the product.

6. Victoria bought $\frac{1}{2}$ pound of fish for dinner. Draw a picture or write an equation to show how much fish she and her brother will get if they divide it evenly between them.

7. $\frac{1}{3} \div 5 = \frac{1}{15}$

   Ⓐ $\frac{1}{3} \times 5$

   Ⓑ $\frac{1}{15} \times \frac{1}{15}$

   Ⓒ $\frac{1}{15} \times \frac{1}{3}$

   Ⓓ $\frac{1}{15} \times 5$

8. $6 \div \frac{1}{4} = 24$

   _____

9. $\frac{1}{3} \div 7 = \frac{1}{21}$

   _____

10. $\frac{1}{8} \div 2 = \frac{1}{16}$

   Ⓐ $\frac{1}{16} \times \frac{1}{8}$

   Ⓑ $\frac{1}{16} \times 8$

   Ⓒ $\frac{1}{16} \times 2$

   Ⓓ $\frac{1}{8} \times 2$

11. $3 \div \frac{1}{5} = 15$

   Ⓐ $15 \times \frac{1}{5}$

   Ⓑ $3 \times \frac{1}{5}$

   Ⓒ 15×3

   Ⓓ 15×5

12. On his math test, Chase wrote that $\frac{1}{6} \div 12 = 2$. What multiplication equation could Chase have used to check his answer?

   _____

   What is the correct answer for Chase's problem?

   _____

13. Aria used the equation $21 \times \frac{1}{3} = 7$ to find out that her answer was correct. What division problem was Aria checking?

   Ⓐ $21 \div \frac{1}{3}$

   Ⓑ $21 \div 7$

   Ⓒ $\frac{1}{3} \div 7$

   Ⓓ $7 \div \frac{1}{3}$

Convert Units
Measurement and Data

DIRECTIONS: Read each problem. Then, choose or write the best answer.

> **Strategy** Use multiplication and division to convert a measurement in one unit to a measurement in another unit.

> **Test Tip** When working with metric units, move the decimal point to the right to convert from a larger unit to a smaller unit, and to the left to convert from a smaller unit to a larger unit.

1. Complete the table of unit conversions.

m	cm
	170
2.5	
3.24	
	1250

2. There are 5,280 feet in 1 mile and 3 feet in 1 yard. How many yards are in 3 miles?
   (A) 5,280
   (B) 1,760
   (C) 47,520
   (D) 2,630

3. Complete the table of unit conversions.

m	cm
2	
	725
0.75	
	3600

4. A jar holds 10 L of liquid. How many 250-mL containers can fill the jar?
   (A) 2,500
   (B) 1,000
   (C) 40
   (D) 400

Write how you found your answer.

_____

_____

5. Complete the table of unit conversions.

g	kg
1000	
	2.5
562	
	12.50

6. Complete the table of unit conversions.

in.	ft.
	3
30	
144	
	6

Convert Units
Measurement and Data

DIRECTIONS: Read each problem. Then, choose or write the best answer.

Strategy Draw a visual model to understand and solve problems converting measurements.

7. Blake needs 2 gallons of water to make a pot of soup. His measuring cup holds 1 cup of water. How many times will Blake have to fill his measuring cup to make his soup? Draw a picture or write an equation in the box to solve the problem.

> 4 quarts = 1 gallon
> 2 pints = 1 quart
> 2 cups = 1 pint

8. Molly wants new carpeting in her bedroom. She measured the length of her room at 12 feet and the width at 10 feet. The carpet she likes is $2.00 a square yard. How much will it cost Molly to carpet her room?

Part A: Convert feet to yards

Length: _____ yards

Width: _____ yards

Part B: Find the area of the room in square yards.

Part C: Find the cost of the carpet. Round your answer to the nearest penny.

9. A cheetah can run at speeds up to 70 miles per hour. At top speed, how long would it take a cheetah to pounce on its prey that is grazing 1,000 feet away?

Part A: Convert miles to feet and hours to minutes.

70 miles = _____ feet

1 hour = _____ minutes

Part B: Convert miles per hour to feet per minute.

Part C: Find the time it would take the cheetah to get to its prey. Round your answer to the nearest hundredth of a second.

Use a Line Plot
Measurement and Data

DIRECTIONS: Use the data to answer the questions.

Strategy Use a line plot to organize and display data so that it is easier to interpret.

Test Tip Read the headings and titles of tables to understand the data in the table. The tally marks in this table represent the number of containers holding each amount of liquid.

Amount of Liquid in Each Container (in L)	
$\frac{1}{8}$ L	| | | | | | |
$\frac{1}{4}$ L	| | | | | | | |
$\frac{1}{3}$ L	| | |
$\frac{1}{2}$ L	| | | | | | | | | |

1. Use the data from the table to complete the line plot.

Amount of Liquid in Each Container

_____

$\frac{1}{8}$ L $\frac{1}{4}$ L $\frac{1}{3}$ L $\frac{1}{2}$ L

2. Which amount of liquid is found in the most containers?

   (A) $\frac{1}{8}$ L

   (B) $\frac{1}{4}$ L

   (C) $\frac{1}{3}$ L

   (D) $\frac{1}{2}$ L

3. Which amount of liquid is found in the least number of containers?

   (A) $\frac{1}{8}$ L

   (B) $\frac{1}{4}$ L

   (C) $\frac{1}{3}$ L

   (D) $\frac{1}{2}$ L

4. Which two equations show how to find the total amount of liquid?

   (A) $\frac{1}{8} + \frac{1}{4} + \frac{1}{3} + \frac{1}{2}$

   (B) $7 + 8 + 3 + 10$

   (C) $\frac{7}{8} + \frac{8}{4} + \frac{3}{3} + \frac{10}{2}$

   (D) $\frac{7}{8} + 2 + 1 + 5$

Use a Line Plot
Measurement and Data

DIRECTIONS: Use the data to answer the questions.

Strategy Read the problem carefully to make sure you know what data to show and interpret on a line plot.

Test Tip Identify the fractions as you read each question.

5. What is the total amount of liquid in the containers?

_____

6. How many containers have less than $\frac{1}{2}$ L of liquid?

(A) 7

(B) 8

(C) 10

(D) 18

7. If you were to combine all of the $\frac{1}{8}$ L containers with all of the $\frac{1}{3}$ L containers, how much liquid would you have?

_____

Write how you found your answer.

_____

_____

_____

8. Use the same number of containers and redistribute them on the line plot below so that each measure is found in the same number of containers.

Amount of Liquid in Each Container

_____

$\frac{1}{8}$ L $\frac{1}{4}$ L $\frac{1}{3}$ L $\frac{1}{2}$ L

Understand Volume
Measurement and Data

DIRECTIONS: Read the questions. Then, choose or write the best answer.

> **Strategy**   Use measurement to answer questions about volume.

> **Test Tip**   Remember, solid shapes are 3-dimensional, so you must use 3 measurements to find their volume.

1. **Which of the following can be measured with volume?**

   (A) how heavy a book is

   (B) how tall a book is

   (C) how thick a book is

   (D) how much space a book takes up

2. **Alex measured the volume of his aquarium. Which of the measurements below could be his answer?**

   (A) 1,500 square inches

   (B) 1,500 inches

   (C) 1,500 cubic ounces

   (D) 1,500 cubic inches

3. **Is it possible to find the volume of an octagon? Why or why not?**

   _____

   _____

   _____

4. **For each shape listed below, write *yes* if it is possible to find the volume. Write *no* if it is not possible. Then, give a reason for each answer.**

   rectangular prism _____

   _____

   sphere _____

   _____

triangle _____

_____

circle _____

_____

> **Test Tip**   A cube with a length of 1 unit, called a "unit cube," is said to have "1 cubic unit" of volume and can be used to measure volume.

5. **Maria filled a shoebox with unit cubes. She found that it took 227 cubes to fill the box completely. How can she write the volume of the box?**

   (A) 227 cubic units

   (B) 227 square units

   (C) 227 units

   (D) 227 blue cubes

Understand Volume
Measurement and Data

Strategy | Visualize the situation described in the problem in your head to help you understand what is happening the problem.

6. Aaron used unit cubes to build a rectangular prism. He laid 3 across, 8 back, and stacked them 4 high. What is the volume of his rectangular prism?

_____

Write how you know.

_____

_____

_____

_____

_____

7. Adam found some bricks in his backyard. Each brick was 1 cubic foot. He stacked them into a cube. There were 5 bricks across, 5 bricks back, and 5 bricks up. How can Adam express the volume of his brick cube?

Ⓐ 15 cubic feet

Ⓑ 5 cubic feet

Ⓒ 50 cubic feet

Ⓓ 125 cubic feet

8. Malik uses unit cubes to build two figures. He makes a figure that is 5 cubes across, 5 cubes back, and 2 cubes up. He then makes a figure that is 10 cubes across, 2 cubes back, and 2 cubes up. Which figure has the greater volume? Tell how you know.

_____

_____

_____

_____

_____

9. Part A: Look at the figure to the right. What is the volume of this prism?

_____

Write how you know.

_____

Part B: What would the volume be if 4 more identical stacks of cubes were added behind this one?

_____

Write how you know.

_____

_____

_____

Find Volume
Measurement and Data

DIRECTIONS: Read each question. Then, choose or write the best answer.

Strategy

Use a formula to find volume. When using a formula, think about what each variable means. Substitute the given number for each variable and perform the operation.
Formulas for Volume:
$V = l \times w \times h$
$V = B \times h$ (B is the area of the base)

Test Tip

The two formulas above actually mean the same thing. You can replace $l \times w$ with B, because the area of the base is found by multiplying the length by the width.

1. Tristan measured his bookshelf. He found that it is 1 foot wide, 3 feet long, and 6 feet tall. What is the volume of Tristan's bookshelf?

   (A) 18 feet

   (B) 10 square feet

   (C) 18 cubic feet

   (D) 10 cubic feet

   Write how you found your answer.

   _____

   _____

2. Mrs. Weinstein has a stack of math books on her desk. One math book has an area of 99 square inches. The stack is 12 inches high. How much space is the stack of math books taking up?

   _____

3. Sydney wants to send a birthday gift to her cousin. She has a box that is 6 inches wide, 6 inches long, and 4 inches deep. Is the box large enough for a gift with a volume of 125 cubic inches?

   _____

   Write how you know.

   _____

   _____

4. Which boxes have a volume larger than this box?

   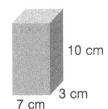
   10 cm
   3 cm
   7 cm

   (A) a box with the side lengths 3 cm, 5 cm, and 12 cm

   (B) a box with the side lengths 8 cm, 4 cm, and 14 cm

   (C) a box with the side lengths 10 cm, 7 cm, and 5 cm

   (D) a box with the side lengths 1 cm, 1 cm, and 25 cm

Find Volume
Measurement and Data

Strategy Draw shapes described in word problems and label measurements given. Use the drawing to solve the problem.

Test Tip If you use more than one prism to create a shape, you can add their individual volumes to find the volume of the whole shape.

5. Julian got an autographed basketball from his favorite team. He wants to put it in a protective box. The basketball has a volume of 456 cubic inches. He went to the store and found 3 protective cases for sports balls.

   Box A is a cube with a side length of 5 inches

   Box B is a cube with a side length of 8 inches

   Box C is a cube with a side length of 10 inches

   Which box should Julian buy for his ball? Why?

   _____

   _____

   _____

6. Mr. and Mrs. Hale have a pool in their backyard. To know what chemicals to put in it, they need to know how much water it holds. The pool is 4 feet deep, 8 feet wide, and 12 feet long. What is the volume of the pool?

   Ⓐ 96 cubic feet

   Ⓑ 32 cubic feet

   Ⓒ 48 cubic feet

   Ⓓ 384 cubic feet

7. One cubic foot of water is equal to about $7\frac{1}{2}$ gallons. One part of the public pool is 6 feet deep, 25 feet long, and 18 feet wide. How many gallons of water can it hold?

   _____

8. Bella found some old boxes around the house and decided to make something out of them. The picture below shows what she made. If the two boxes on top are congruent and the bottom box is a cube, what is the volume of the entire figure?

   _____

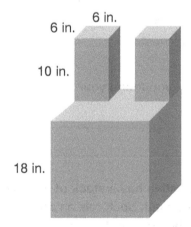

6 in.

6 in.

6 in.

10 in.

18 in.

Graph Points
Geometry

DIRECTIONS: Use the coordinate grid to answer the questions.

Strategy

Graph data by plotting points on the coordinate grid. Each point is identified by an ordered pair written in the form (x, y). So, the first number in the pair corresponds to a point on the x (horizontal) axis, and the second number corresponds to a point on the y (vertical) axis.

Test Tip

When identifying points on a coordinate grid, always start at the origin $(0, 0)$. Move along the x-axis, and then, along the y-axis. Count the lines on the grid, not the spaces.

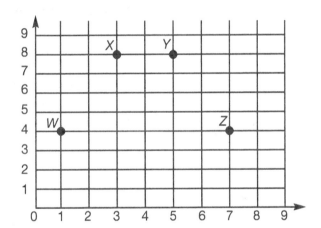

1. **What point is at (5, 8)?**

   (A) W

   (B) X

   (C) Y

   (D) Z

2. **Write the ordered pair for point W.**

   _____

3. **Imagine that this coordinate grid was a map. How would you give somebody directions to get from point W to point X staying on the lines?**

   _____

   _____

4. **Starting at point Z, travel 3 lines down and 4 lines to the left. At what ordered pair did you stop?**

   (A) (3, 7)

   (B) (7, 3)

   (C) (1, 3)

   (D) (3, 1)

5. **If you start at point X and move 2 down, 4 to the right, and 2 down, where do you end up?**

   (A) W

   (B) Y

   (C) Z

   (D) the origin

Name _____ Date _____

Math

Graph Points
Geometry

Strategy Always plot points on the grid the same way you identify them. Start at the origin, move along the *x*-axis. Then, move along the *y*-axis.

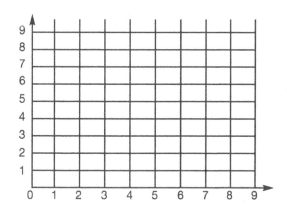

6. Plot the following points on the coordinate grid above.

S (4, 3)   T (0, 7)

U (6, 5)   V (9, 0)

7. Write directions explaining how to move from point *T* to point *U*.

_____

_____

DIRECTIONS: Read the following sentences and use them to answer questions 8–11.

Imagine you are in a city that is organized in a grid pattern. The center of the city is the origin (0, 0). As you travel north or east, the block numbers increase. As you move south and west, the block numbers decrease.

8. Starting in the center of the city, imagine you walk 17 blocks north and 12 blocks west. What are the coordinates of the corner you are standing on?

Ⓐ (17, 12)

Ⓑ (-12, 17)

Ⓒ (0, 0)

Ⓓ (12, 0)

Write how you know.

_____

_____

9. From where you are now, walk 9 blocks east and 2 blocks south. What coordinate are you at now?

_____

10. The grocery store is located at the coordinates (5, 8). Give directions from where you are now to the grocery store.

_____

_____

11. Now, give directions to get back to the center of the city.

_____

_____

12. Look at the coordinate grid. Which sequence of ordered pairs would allow you to move from the school to the library?

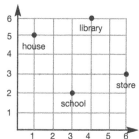

Ⓐ (2,3), (3,3), (4,3), (5,3), (6,3), (6,4)

Ⓑ (3,2), (3,3), (3,4), (3,5), (2,5), (1,5)

Ⓒ (3,2), (3,3), (3,4), (3,5), (3,6), (4,6)

Ⓓ (2,3), (2,4), (2,5), (2,6), (3,6), (4,6)

Math

Classify 2-D Shapes
Geometry

DIRECTIONS: Name and draw the described polygon.

Strategy   Use the characteristics of polygons to classify them.

Test Tip   Remember that two-dimensional shapes are categorized by their characteristics, such as number of sides and angles and whether they have parallel and perpendicular lines.

1. Polygon with three equal sides

Shape: _____

2. Polygon with opposite sides equal and four right angles

Shape: _____

3. Polygon with three sides of different lengths

Shape: _____

4. Polygon with four sides equal, opposite sides parallel, and four angles equal

Shape: _____

5. Which of the following shapes is NOT a quadrilateral?

Ⓐ parallelogram

Ⓑ pentagon

Ⓒ rhombus

Ⓓ square

Write how you know.

_____

_____

Classify 2-D Shapes
Geometry

DIRECTIONS: Read each question. Then, choose or write the best answer.

Strategy | Read each description carefully and use the characteristics described in the problem and the characteristics of shapes to sketch the shape. Use the sketch to solve the problem.

6. I am a quadrilateral.

   I am a parallelogram.

   I have 4 right angles.

   My opposite sides are congruent.

   Who am I?

   _____

7. I am a quadrilateral.

   I am a parallelogram.

   I have no right angles.

   All of my sides are congruent.

   Who am I?

   _____

8. I am a 3-sided polygon.

   I have no congruent sides.

   I have a right angle.

   Who am I?

   _____

9. Place the names of the shapes in the graphic organizer from the most general name at the top to the most specific name at the bottom.

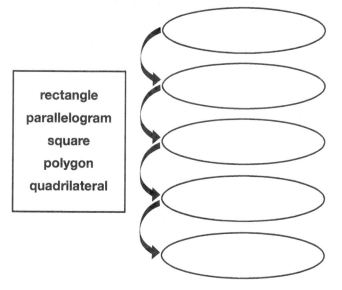

rectangle
parallelogram
square
polygon
quadrilateral

10. Which of these terms describes a rhombus? Choose three.

    (A) polygon

    (B) square

    (C) parallelogram

    (D) quadrilateral

Strategy Review

Strategy   Apply prior knowledge and basic operations to solve problems.

You can use what you know about number relationships and computation skills to solve real-world problems.

EXAMPLE
Miss Lacy bought 6 pounds of apples at $1.99 per pound, 2 cartons of eggs at $2.69 per dozen, and 5 cans of cat food at $1.39 each. She had a coupon for $0.50 off each can of cat food. How much was Miss Lacy's total bill before tax?

First, write an expression to model the problem.
$(6 \times 1.99) + (2 \times 2.69) + 5 (1.39 - .50)$

Next, use order of operations to evaluate the expression.

Evaluate parentheses first: $(11.94) + (5.38) + 5 (0.89) =$
Multiply from left to right: $(11.94) + (5.38) + 4.45 =$
Add from left to right: $11.94 + 5.38 + 4.45 = \$21.77$

Mis Lacy's bill was $21.77.

1. Miles has $475. He spends $125 on new school clothes. Then, three of his relatives each give him $25 for his birthday. Finally, Miles divides the remaining money into three equal amounts. He puts one part into his college fund and one part into his savings account. He keeps the third part. Write and evaluate an expression to show how much money Miles has.

_____

2. On Thursday, Alexandra's teacher assigned her to read a book by the following Tuesday. The book has 450 pages. She thinks she can read 75 pages on weekdays and 150 pages each on Saturday and Sunday. Does Alexandra have enough time to finish the book if she starts reading on Thursday? Write and evaluate an expression to find the answer.

_____

How did the strategy help you answer these questions?

_____

_____

_____

_____

Strategy Review

Strategy Look for key words in word problems that help you know which operation to use.

EXAMPLE

In a game of *Go Fish*, each card that a player has on the table gives the player points. Each card left in the player's hand takes points away. Cards 2–9 are worth 5 points each. Tens and face cards are worth 10 points each. Aces are worth 15 points each.

Jordan and Carson were playing a game of *Go Fish*. Carson had four twos, four fives, and four sevens down on the table. He had an ace and two kings left in his hand. How many points does Carson have?

First, identify key words that tell you what operations to use.

> The words "gives the player points" suggest addition.
> The words "takes points away" suggest subtraction.

Then, write an expression to represent the situation.

> $5(4 + 4 + 4) - (15 + 2 \times 10)$

Evaluate parentheses. If there are multiple operations within parentheses, multiply or divide from left to right first. Then, add or subtract from left to right.

> $5(12) - 35$

Perform all multiplication and division, working from left to right. Separate each calculation as needed.

> $60 - 35$

Add or subtract from left to right.

> 25

Carson has 25 points.

1. Julia played a round of mini golf. In the first 5 holes, she scored 2 over par, 3 under par, 1 over par, 3 over par, and 2 under par. Where is Julia's score in regards to par after the first 5 holes?

   (A) 1 under par

   (B) 1 over par

   (C) 3 over par

   (D) 5 under par

2. Colin has to earn his computer time. He earns 15 minutes for every 15 minutes of homework he does and for each chore he does. He loses 15 minutes every time he argues with his sister. On Saturday, Colin read for 15 minutes, cleaned the bathroom, argued with his sister 3 times, and did his math homework for half an hour. How much computer time did Colin earn or lose for Saturday?

   (A) earned 15 minutes

   (B) lost 15 minutes

   (C) earned 30 minutes

   (D) lost 30 minutes

Strategy

Use drawings, graphs, or number lines to understand and solve a problem.

3. A mountain like Mt. Everest cannot be climbed all at once. A climber must get his body used to the altitude, so he will climb up and then, climb back down again a few times to get used to the altitude. If a climber climbed 1,000 feet, then descended 500 feet, then climbed again 1,200 feet and descended 700 feet, how high would he have climbed? Make a drawing that helps you solve the problem.

Strategy Review

<table>
<tr><td>**Strategy**</td><td>Organize and display data in order to interpret it.</td></tr>
</table>

EXAMPLE

A fast-food restaurant tracks the hamburgers its customers order. On a given day, customers order the following sizes (in pounds):

$$\frac{1}{4}, \frac{1}{2}, \frac{1}{2}, \frac{1}{3}, \frac{1}{4}, \frac{1}{4}, \frac{1}{3}, \frac{1}{2}, \frac{1}{2}, \frac{1}{4}, \frac{1}{2}$$

Use a line plot to organize the data.
First, label the line plot with the range of data.

$$\frac{1}{4} \qquad\qquad \frac{1}{3} \qquad\qquad \frac{1}{2}$$

Then, add Xs to show the data.

```
                              X
        X                     X
        X                     X
        X           X         X
        X           X         X
       _____
        1/4         1/3        1/2
```

EXAMPLE

A farmer has 42 animals on his farm. Thirteen of the animals are chickens. He also has 5 horses, 7 pigs, and some cows. The farmer grows and sells about 100 pounds of corn and 50 pounds of pumpkins per month. How many cows does the farmer have?

What is the given information?
   A farmer has 42 animals. He has 13 chickens, 5 horses, and 7 cows. He grows and sells 100 pounds of corn and 50 pounds of pumpkins each month.

What are you being asked to find?
   the number of cows on the farm

Is any of the given information extra, or not needed?
   Yes, we do not need to know the amount of corn and pumpkins he grows and sells.

Now, you can use your line plot to answer questions about the data.

1. How many people ordered hamburgers? _____

2. What size hamburger was ordered most often?

   _____

3. What size hamburger was ordered least often?

   _____

<table>
<tr><td>**Test Tip**</td></tr>
<tr><td>Read word problems carefully to identify the given information and what you are being asked to find.</td></tr>
</table>

4. 112 teachers and students went to the museum. They arrived at 9:30 A.M. The teachers and students were broken up into four equal groups. How many teachers and students were in each group?

What is the given information?

_____

_____

What are you being asked to find?

_____

Is any of the given information extra, or not needed?

_____

_____

Strategy Review

Strategy Use rules, properties, or formulas to solve problems.

EXAMPLE

Ruby received a package in the mail that came in a 12 in. by 13 in. by 7 in. box. Use the formula for volume, $V = l \times w \times h$ or $V = Bh$, to find the volume of the carton.

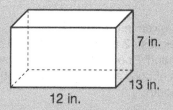

7 in.

13 in.

12 in.

First, write the formula for the volume of a right rectangular prism.
$V = l \times w \times h$

Put the measurements into the formula.
$V = l \times w \times h = 12 \times 13 \times 7 = 1,092$

The volume of the box is 1,092 in.^{3}

1. Ruby has a chest in her room that is 18 inches tall, 4 feet long, and 2 feet wide. What is the volume of the chest?

2. Hudson is painting his wall. The wall is 10 feet long and 8 feet high. What is the area that Hudson will be painting?

   (A) 18 ft^2

   (B) 80 ft^2

   (C) 180 ft^2

   (D) 38 ft^2

3. Hudson wants to put a border all around his room. If all of Hudson's walls are the same dimensions, how long must the border be to fit all the way around the room?

   (A) 10 feet

   (B) 25 feet

   (C) 40 feet

   (D) 50 feet

Quote Text to Support Inferences
Reading: Literature

DIRECTIONS: Read the story. Then, answer the questions.

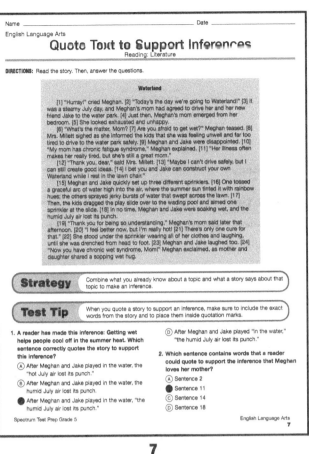

Waterland

[1] "Hurray!" cried Meghan. [2] "Today's the day we're going to Waterland!" [3] It was a steamy July day, and Meghan's mom had agreed to drive her and her new friend Jake to the water park. [4] Just then, Meghan's mom emerged from her bedroom. [5] She looked exhausted and unhappy.

[6] "What's the matter, Mom? [7] Are you afraid to get wet?" Meghan teased. [8] Mrs. Millett sighed as she informed the kids that she was feeling unwell and far too tired to drive to the water park safely. [9] Meghan and Jake were disappointed. [10] "My mom has chronic fatigue syndrome," Meghan explained. [11] "Her illness often makes her really tired, but she's still a great mom."

[12] "Thank you, dear," said Mrs. Millett. [13] "Maybe I can't drive safely, but I can still create good ideas. [14] I bet you and Jake can construct your own Waterland while I rest in the lawn chair."

[15] Meghan and Jake quickly set up three different sprinklers. [16] One tossed a graceful arc of water high into the air, where the summer sun tinted it with rainbow hues; the others sprayed jerky bursts of water that swept across the lawn. [17] Then, the kids dragged the play slide over to the wading pool and aimed one sprinkler at the slide. [18] In no time, Meghan and Jake were soaking wet, and the humid July air lost its punch.

[19] "Thank you for being so understanding," Meghan's mom said later that afternoon. [20] "I feel better now, but I'm really hot! [21] There's only one cure for that." [22] She stood under the sprinkler wearing all of her clothes and laughing, until she was drenched from head to foot. [23] Meghan and Jake laughed too. [24] "Now you have chronic wet syndrome, Mom!" Meghan exclaimed, as mother and daughter shared a sopping wet hug.

Strategy — Combine what you already know about a topic and what a story says about that topic to make an inference.

Test Tip — When you quote a story to support an inference, make sure to include the exact words from the story and to place them inside quotation marks.

1. A reader has made this inference: Getting wet helps people cool off in the summer heat. Which sentence correctly quotes the story to support this inference?
   (A) After Meghan and Jake played in the water, the "hot July air lost its punch."
   (B) After Meghan and Jake played in the water, the humid July air lost its punch.
   ● After Meghan and Jake played in the water, "the humid July air lost its punch."
   (D) After Meghan and Jake played "in the water," "the humid July air lost its punch."

2. Which sentence contains words that a reader could quote to support the inference that Meghan loves her mother?
   (A) Sentence 2
   ● Sentence 11
   (C) Sentence 14
   (D) Sentence 18

English Language Arts **7**

Quote Text to Support Inferences
Reading: Literature

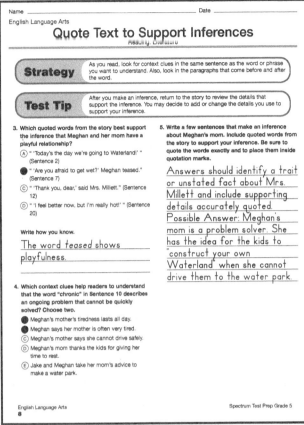

Strategy — As you read, look for context clues in the same sentence as the word or phrase you want to understand. Also, look in the paragraphs that come before and after the word.

Test Tip — After you make an inference, return to the story to review the details that support the inference. You may decide to add or change the details you use to support your inference.

3. Which quoted words from the story best support the inference that Meghan and her mom have a playful relationship?
   (A) " 'Today's the day we're going to Waterland!' " (Sentence 2)
   ● " 'Are you afraid to get wet?' Meghan teased." (Sentence 7)
   (C) " 'Thank you, dear,' said Mrs. Millett." (Sentence 12)
   (D) " 'I feel better now, but I'm really hot!' " (Sentence 20)

Write how you know.

The word *teased* shows playfulness.

4. Which context clues help readers to understand that the word "chronic" in Sentence 10 describes an ongoing problem that cannot be quickly solved? Choose two.
   ● Meghan's mother's tiredness lasts all day.
   ● Meghan says her mother is often very tired.
   (C) Meghan's mother says she cannot drive safely.
   (D) Meghan's mom thanks the kids for giving her time to rest.
   (E) Jake and Meghan take her mom's advice to make a water park.

5. Write a few sentences that make an inference about Meghan's mom. Include quoted words from the story to support your inference. Be sure to quote the words exactly and to place them inside quotation marks.

Answers should identify a trait or unstated fact about Mrs. Millett and include supporting details accurately quoted. Possible Answer: Meghan's mom is a problem solver. She has the idea for the kids to "construct your own Waterland" when she cannot drive them to the water park.

Spectrum Test Prep Grade 5

Determine Theme and Summarize Text
Reading: Literature

DIRECTIONS: Read the story. Then, answer the questions.

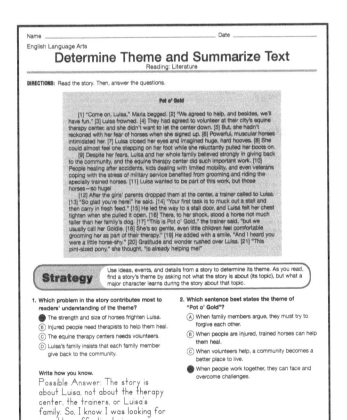

Pot o' Gold

[1] "Come on, Luisa," Marla begged. [2] "We agreed to help, and besides, we'll have fun." [3] Luisa frowned. [4] They had agreed to volunteer at their city's equine therapy center, and she didn't want to let the center down. [5] But, she hadn't reckoned with her fear of horses when she signed up. [6] Powerful, muscular horses intimidated her. [7] Luisa closed her eyes and imagined huge, hard hooves. [8] She could almost feel one stepping on her foot while she reluctantly pulled her boots on.

[9] Despite her fears, Luisa and her whole family believed strongly in giving back to the community, and the equine therapy center did such important work. [10] People healing after accidents, kids dealing with limited mobility, and even veterans coping with the stress of military service benefited from grooming and riding the specially trained horses. [11] Luisa wanted to be part of this work, but those horses—so huge!

[12] After the girls' parents dropped them at the center, a trainer called to Luisa. [13] "So glad you're here!" he said. [14] "Your first task is to muck out a stall and then carry in fresh feed." [15] He led the way to a stall door, and Luisa felt her chest tighten when she pulled it open. [16] There, to her shock, stood a horse not much taller than her family's dog. [17] "This is Pot o' Gold," the trainer said, "but we usually call her Goldie. [18] She's so gentle, we like children feel comfortable grooming her as part of their therapy. [19] He added with a smile, "And I heard you were a little horse-shy." [20] Gratitude and wonder rushed over Luisa. [21] "This pint-sized pony," she thought, "is already helping me!"

Strategy — Use ideas, events, and details from a story to determine its theme. As you read, find a story's theme by asking not what the story is about (its topic), but what a major character learns during the story about that topic.

1. Which problem in the story contributes most to readers' understanding of the theme?
   ● The strength and size of horses frighten Luisa.
   (B) Injured people need therapists to help them heal.
   (C) The equine therapy centers needs volunteers.
   (D) Luisa's family insists that each family member give back to the community.

2. Which sentence best states the theme of "Pot o' Gold"?
   (A) When family members argue, they must try to forgive each other.
   (B) When people are injured, trained horses can help them heal.
   (C) When volunteers help, a community becomes a better place to live.
   ● When people work together, they can face and overcome challenges.

Write how you know.
Possible Answer: The story is about Luisa, not about the therapy center, the trainers, or Luisa's family. So, I know I was looking for a problem affecting Luisa.

English Language Arts **9**

Determine Theme and Summarize Text
Reading: Literature

Strategy — While reading, identify the main idea and then details that support the main idea. Underline the main idea and details or write them down. Use them to summarize the story.

3. Write the sentence that supports the theme with Luisa's actions.

Possible Answers: Despite her fears, Luisa and her whole family believed strongly in giving back to community, and the equine therapy center did such important work. Luisa wanted to be part of this work, but those horses—so huge!

4. Which action in the story best demonstrates the theme?
   (A) Luisa cleans out Goldie's stall and feeds her.
   (B) Marla pushes Luisa to help at the therapy center.
   ● The trainer ensures that Luisa works with a little horse.
   (D) Luisa's parents set a good example by volunteering in the community.

5. Which detail from the story must be included in a clear and complete summary?
   (A) The little horse's name is Goldie.
   (B) Marla is comfortable working with horses.
   ● Luisa decides to volunteer despite her fears.
   (D) People healing from accidents may use equine therapy.

Test Tip — Include only the important plot points and major characters in the summary of a story. Leave out less important characters and details the author includes to enhance the story.

6. Which character should be included in a complete summary of the story? Choose all that apply.
   (A) Goldie's trainer
   (B) Luisa's parents
   ● Luisa
   ● Marla

Write how you know.
Possible Answer: The story is about Luisa. Marla is the character who brings Luisa to the equine therapy center, so she is important.

7. Is Goldie important to mention in a summary? Explain why or why not.
Possible Answer: Yes. Goldie is important because the small horse helps Luisa get over her fear of horses.

8. Write a summary of the events in "Pot o' Gold."
Summaries should include the major characters and events. Possible Answer: Luisa's fear of horses makes it hard for her to volunteer at an equine therapy center, but a miniature horse named Goldie gives her the confidence to face and begin to overcome her fear.

Spectrum Test Prep Grade 5

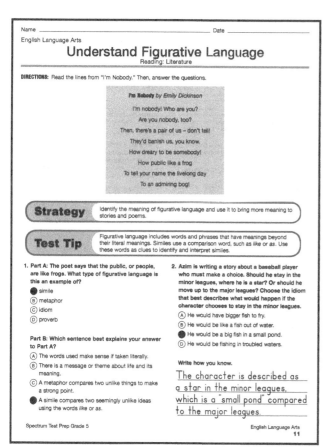

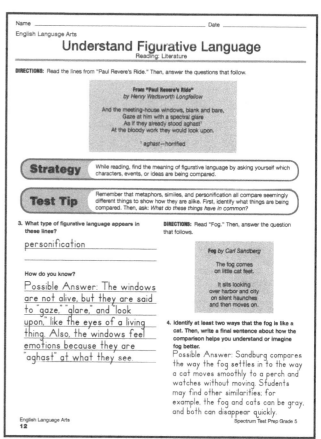

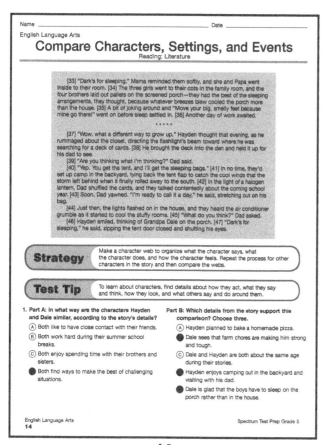

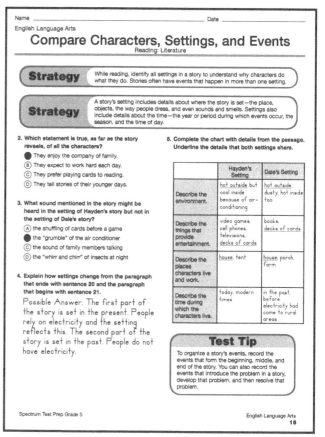

Compare Characters, Settings, and Events
Reading: Literature

Strategy — As you read, make inferences about what the characters think of each other. Base these inferences on not only what they say and do, but also on what you already know from your own experience.

6. Which statement about a problem that must be solved is supported by the story?
- ● Hayden's plans are spoiled by a strong summer storm.
- Ⓑ Dale's family has a hard time enduring the summer heat.
- Ⓒ Hayden and Dale find the routine of summer days boring.
- Ⓓ Hayden's mother is away at a conference during a power outage.

7. Which two sentences are evidence that Hayden no longer feels concerned about the power outage?
- Ⓐ Sentence 20
- ● Sentence 37
- ● Sentence 44
- Ⓓ Sentence 47

8. Hayden's dad is a positive, happy person. Is this a fair inference to make? Explain why or why not.

Possible Answer: Yes; He doesn't get upset about the power outage. He tells Hayden's mom that everything is fine. He helps Hayden find other things to do during the outage.

9. Which inference is supported in the ending of the story?
- ● The power outage helped Hayden become closer to his grandfather.
- Ⓑ Hayden's dad was very worried and unhappy about the power outage.
- Ⓒ Spending time outdoors is something that was only done in the past.
- Ⓓ Electricity is the most important technology we have today.

10. Characters from three generations have roles in the story. Use details from the story to describe what Hayden learns from other characters.

Possible Answer: Hayden uses memories of his grandfather's stories to learn how to cope with surprising situations and how to be happy with simple pleasures. Hayden also learns from his father to find a solution to the problem of the power outage.

English Language Arts
16

Spectrum Test Prep Grade 5

16

Explain Text Structure
Reading: Literature

Strategy — Use structural elements of a drama to draw out more meaning.

Test Tip — Characters and setting are often identified before the play's lines start. Dialogue markers tell who is speaking. Stage directions—descriptions of what characters do and how they move and speak—are often in italics and inside parentheses.

1. What do the stage directions suggest about the personality of Mr. Cratchit?
- Ⓐ He is a clever man who does well as a clerk.
- ● He is a quiet man who finds his employer intimidating.
- Ⓒ He is a sorrowful man who prefers a cold and dark room.
- Ⓓ He is a cheerful man who likes his employer despite his grumpy ways.

2. Write the stage direction that helps readers most clearly imagine the weather in which this action takes place.

(a frigid gust of wind and a sprinkling of snow accompany him)

3. What detail can readers find in the story structure that makes Scrooge's refusal to burn coal to heat the room even more confusing?
- ● The list of players says that Scrooge is wealthy.
- Ⓑ Fred closes the office door to keep the cold out.
- Ⓒ Fred's second speech suggests that Cratchit is already bundled up.
- Ⓓ The description of the setting gives the place and time as 1840s London.

Test Tip — Make inferences about the characters based not only on what they say, but also on what the stage directions suggest about how they say it and what they do.

4. If you were directing this scene, you would give instructions to the actors on how to play each role. Review the scene. Then, write notes to the actor playing Scrooge on what facial expressions he should use, how he should move, and how he should say each line. Draw on the structure of the play to support your instructions.

Possible Answer: Scrooge is a stingy and unkind man. When you say his lines, frown and scowl. Scrooge is working in the cold. Sit hunched over and shiver. Say the first speech in an angry and threatening voice. Say his second speech as if he seems proud of himself for being unwilling to spend money to stay warm.

English Language Arts
18

Spectrum Test Prep Grade 5

18

Analyze a Poem
Reading: Literature

DIRECTIONS: Read the poem. Then, answer the questions.

The Rainy Day by Henry Wadsworth Longfellow

The day is cold, and dark, and dreary;
It rains, and the wind is never weary;
The vine still clings to the mouldering[1] wall,
But at every gust the dead leaves fall,
And the day is dark and dreary.

My life is cold, and dark, and dreary;
It rains, and the wind is never weary;
My thoughts still cling to the mouldering Past,
But the hopes of youth fall thick in the blast,
And the days are dark and dreary.

Be still, sad heart! and cease repining[2];
Behind the clouds is the sun still shining;
Thy fate is the common fate of all,
Into each life some rain must fall,
Some days must be dark and dreary.

[1]mouldering—crumbling; decaying
[2]repining—complaining

Strategy — Use structural elements of a poem to draw out more meaning. Although poems are shorter and have a unique format, they often have the same elements as fiction—characters, problems or conflict, setting, and theme.

Test Tip — Whether you read a story or a poem, you can often identify a conflict and a resolution by asking these questions: *What does the speaker or character want that he can't get? How does the speaker either get the thing he wants or decide to do without it?*

1. Which statement summarizes the conflict and resolution in the poem?
- Ⓐ The speaker is annoyed because the day is rainy until he sees the sun come out again.
- Ⓑ The speaker is upset that his house's walls need repairing until he realizes that he can fix them.
- ● The speaker is sad about getting older until he remembers that everyone has sad days.
- Ⓓ The speaker is enjoying the cool autumn weather until he remembers that summer will come soon.

2. Part A: Which phrase describes the poem's tone in the first two stanzas?
- Ⓐ alarmed and restless
- Ⓑ irritated and confused
- Ⓒ thoughtful and content
- ● gloomy and distressed

Spectrum Test Prep Grade 5

English Language Arts
19

19

Analyze a Poem
Reading: Literature

Strategy — Reread a story or poem and focus on the descriptive details to form a picture in your mind.

Test Tip — Paying attention to details in a poem and visualizing those details will help you focus on the tone of the poem.

Part B: Which sentence in the third stanza marks a change in tone?
- ● "Behind the clouds is the sun still shining"
- Ⓑ "Thy fate is the common fate of all"
- Ⓒ "Into each life some rain must fall"
- Ⓓ "Some days must be dark and dreary"

3. How does the title of the poem "The Rainy Day" fit with the tone?
- Ⓐ it describes sunny weather
- Ⓑ it tells who the narrator is
- ● it describes a dreary, rainy day
- Ⓓ it tells what the poem is about

4. Which words and phrases show how the narrator, or speaker, feels?

My life is cold, and dark, and dreary; Be still, sad heart!

5. How would the poem be different if the poet described a bright, sunny day? Think about meaning, tone, and mood.

Possible Answer: The meaning would be positive. The poem's mood would be happy. The tone would be happy.

Test Tip — When a story or poem includes visuals, such as drawings, the visuals usually serve a purpose. Examine the illustrations to analyze how they support, extend, or explain something about the setting, characters, or plot of the story or poem.

6. Imagine you are an artist who is asked to create two illustrations for this poem. Describe the illustrations you would create to capture the tone of the poem. Explain how the illustrations would support, extend, or explain something about the poem's setting, speaker, or conflict.

Descriptions of illustrations should include one that is dreary and gray for stanzas 1 and 2 and one that shows the sunlight for stanza 3. Students should explain at least one way in which the illustrations support, extend, or explain something about the poem's setting, speaker, or conflict.

English Language Arts
20

Spectrum Test Prep Grade 5

20

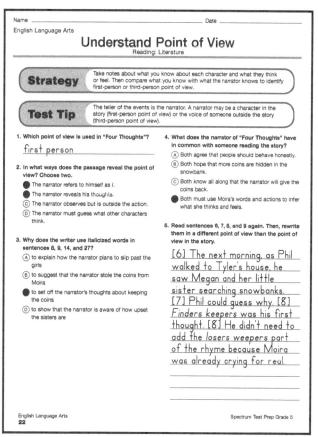

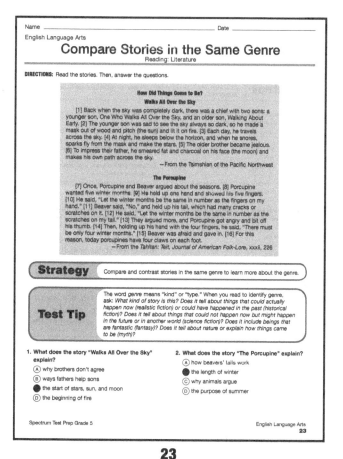

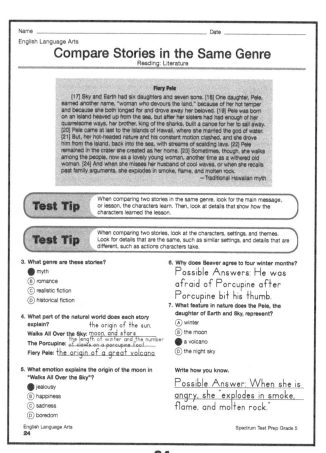

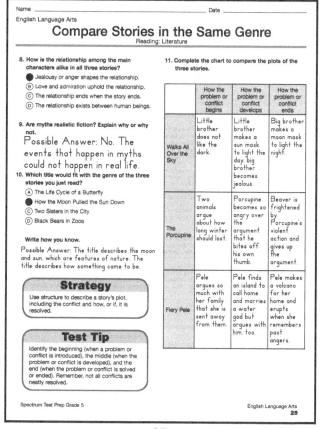

Compare Stories in the Same Genre
Reading: Literature

12. Which statement expresses a theme that each story supports?
- Ⓐ Forceful action solves many problems.
- Ⓑ Family members forgive each other's faults.
- ● People have trouble living together in peace.
- Ⓓ The world of nature is full of unexplained mysteries.

Write how you know.

Possible Answer: In all three stories, the characters did not get along with each other.

13. Stories such as these were often told to young listeners to teach a lesson about expected behavior. Choose one of the stories and explain the lesson you think young listeners might be expected to learn.

Possible Answer for "Fiery Pele": Conflict, argument, and anger lead to destruction and upheaval. Pele wants to have the people she loves with her and seems lonely, but she can never live happily with them for long and either drives them away or is driven away by them.

14. If you wrote a myth, which elements would you include? Choose all that apply.
- ● characters
- ● features of nature
- ● a conflict
- Ⓓ realistic events

Write how you know.

Possible Answer: A myth has characters and a conflict. They are about features of nature. The events could not happen in real life.

15. How can comparing stories in the same genre help you understand the genre?

Possible Answer: Comparing characters, settings, and themes helps readers see what features appear in each story. Knowing what features are presented in a genre helps readers identify them and understand them.

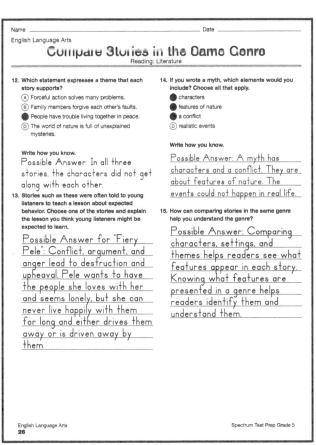

Quote Text to Support Inferences
Reading: Informational Text

DIRECTIONS: Read the article. Then, answer the questions.

Assault of the Everlasting Jellies

[1] They're tiny—about the size of a little finger nail. [2] They're soft—they'd be in trouble among pedestrians. [3] Yet, a species of sea life nicknamed "immortal jellyfish" is making its move on the world's oceans. [4] The scientific name of this creature is a mouthful: *Turritopsis dohrnii*.

[5] If that name sounds a little like "topsy-turvy," it fits. [6] These jellies are highly successful in the ocean for several reasons. [7] First, they traverse distances quickly, perhaps attached to cargo ships' hulls or floating inside the ballast water that helps keep ships upright. [8] Second, they adapt to new environments quickly. [9] For example, these jellies grow different numbers of tentacles in different water temperatures.

[10] However, their most amazing survival trick is what earns them the nickname "immortal." [11] When under stress—when there's not enough food or another hazard arises—every cell in an adult jelly transforms into a younger version of itself. [12] That's right: These jellies can age backward into the blobs from which they were born. [13] Colonies of these jelly blobs, or cysts, can then spawn hundreds of new jellies, each essentially a copy of the blob that spawned it. [14] Scientists are studying how these jellies' genes switch on and off. [15] In the meantime, swarms of the highly successful creatures float the world's oceans, reproducing as they go.

Strategy Make inferences by using facts from the passage and information you already know. Put the two together to create a new idea.

Test Tip Use details from the text to support inferences.

1. Which sentence from the passage supports the inference that the jellies' ability to "age backward" is rare among living things?
- Ⓐ Sentence 3, which explains why their nickname is "immortal jellyfish"
- Ⓑ Sentence 5, which says that their scientific name "sounds a little like 'topsy-turvy'"
- ● Sentence 10, which calls this ability a "most amazing survival trick"
- Ⓓ Sentence 15, which shows that this ability has led to "swarms of the highly successful creatures"

2. Which sentence could be quoted to support the inference that a creature's ability to adapt to new surroundings affects whether it lives or dies?
- Ⓐ Sentence 6
- ● Sentence 9
- Ⓒ Sentence 13
- Ⓓ Sentence 14

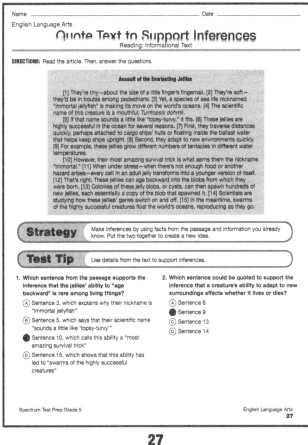

Quote Text to Support Inferences
Reading: Informational Text

Strategy Make inferences by identifying the main idea of the passage. Then, think about what you already know about the topic.

Test Tip It is important to use details exactly as they appear in the passage to support an inference. Read the passage carefully.

3. Which word from the passage describes a kind of motion and comes from a Latin prefix meaning "across" and a Latin root meaning "to turn"?
- ● traverse, in Sentence 7
- Ⓑ tentacles, in Sentence 9
- Ⓒ transforms, in Sentence 11
- Ⓓ colonies, in Sentence 13

4. Which sentence from the passage tells the meaning of *adapt* in sentence 8?
- Ⓐ Sentence 7
- ● Sentence 9
- Ⓒ Sentence 11
- Ⓓ Sentence 13

Write how you know.

Possible Answer: The sentence tells how jellies grow tentacles depending on the temperature of the water.

What does *adapt* mean?

Possible Answer: to change so it's easier to live in a particular place.

Test Tip When looking for context clues, read for words or phrases that may rename, explain, or define the word you don't know.

5. Which phrases in the context surrounding the words "spawn" and "spawned" (Sentence 13) renames or defines a biological activity and provides a clue to the meaning of "spawn"? Choose all that apply.
- Ⓐ "when there's not enough food"
- ● "from which they were born"
- ● "each essentially a copy of the blob"
- Ⓓ "how these jellies' genes switch on and off"
- Ⓔ "reproducing as they go"

Strategy After you make an inference, reread the passage to identify details that clearly support the inference.

6. A reader has made this inference after reading "Assault of the Everlasting Jellies": *Swarms of these jellyfish are spreading through the oceans and threatening marine ecosystems.* Does the passage support this inference? Explain your answer.

Possible Answer: No, the passage does not support this inference. Though there is evidence in the passage that the population numbers of this jellyfish are on the rise and the swarms are growing successfully, there is no phrase or sentence in the passage that could be quoted to support the inference that these swarms are in any way a threat to marine ecosystems.

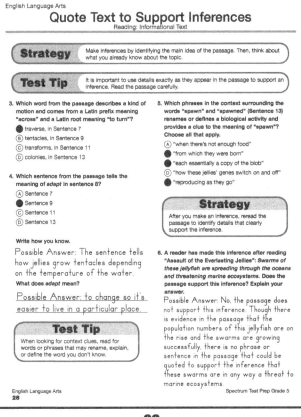

Summarize Using Main Ideas and Details
Reading: Informational Text

DIRECTIONS: Read the passage. Then, answer the questions.

Like No One Else's

[1] Fans of cop shows on television know the drill: When investigators arrive at the crime scene, they are careful not to touch anything. [2] Wearing gloves, they move gingerly around the room, dusting with powder to find fingerprints. [3] If they find prints on a weapon, they are relieved. [4] If they can match the fingerprints to those stored in a database, they may know who committed the crime.

[5] People have known for centuries that fingerprints are unique to individuals. [6] Not even identical twins have matching fingerprints. [7] The ridges, whorls, and loops that mark our fingers (and toes) belong to each of us alone. [8] And, with the exception of scars, our fingerprints remain the same our whole lives.

[9] In the past, fingerprints and palm prints were used as signatures, especially important in past times when only a few people needed to learn to read and write. [10] Historians have even found some artworks marked with their creator's prints. [11] However, it was not until the late 1880s that fingerprints were first matched with people in criminal cases, and even then, progress was slow. [12] It's one thing to know that each person's prints identify him or her. [13] It's another to build files of prints to check against prints found at a crime scene.

[14] In 1924, the United States Congress set up a section of the Federal Bureau of Investigation to collect and file fingerprints. [15] For decades, they were kept on cards, and in fact, several hundred million fingerprint cards are still on file with the FBI. [16] Today, computer databases have made matching fingerprints much easier and faster.

Strategy Use structure to summarize a passage. Identify a main idea for each paragraph of an informational passage. Then, list these main ideas to create a quick outline. Use your outline to summarize.

1. Which statement best states the main idea of the entire passage?
- Ⓐ Fingerprints once served as signatures.
- Ⓑ Millions of fingerprints are on file in this country.
- ● Fingerprints can be used to identify individuals.
- Ⓓ Toe prints and palm prints are also unique to individuals.

2. Which statement best states the main idea of the second paragraph?
- Ⓐ Twins don't have matching fingerprints.
- Ⓑ Fingerprints remain the same our whole lives.
- Ⓒ In the past, fingerprints were used as signatures.
- ● Fingerprints are unique to individuals.

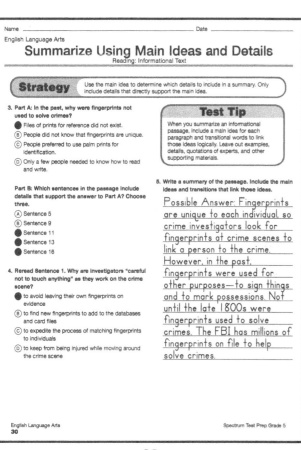

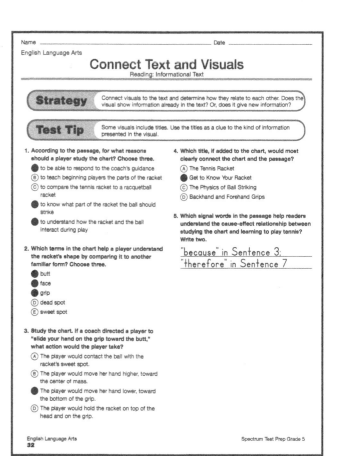

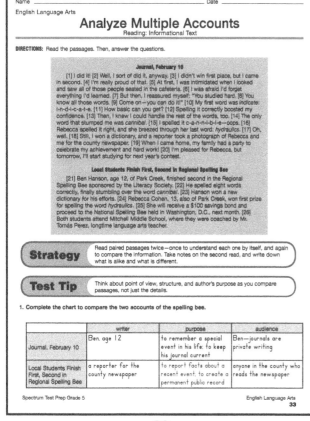

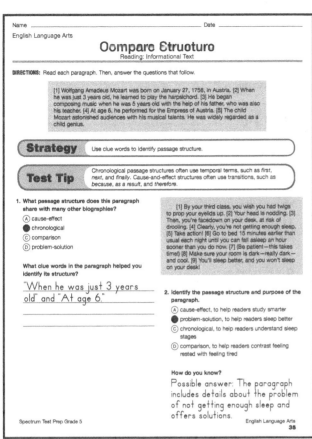

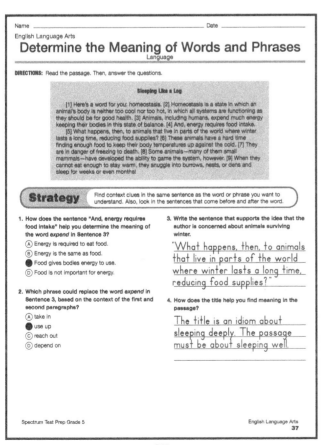

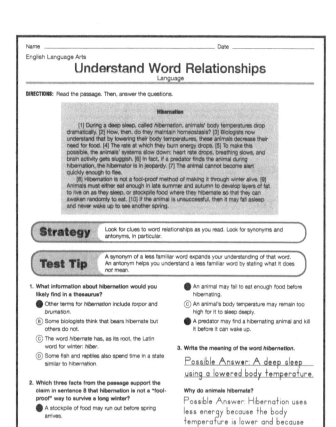

Page 39

Name _____ Date _____

English Language Arts

Understand Word Relationships
Language

DIRECTIONS: Read the passage. Then, answer the questions.

Hibernation

[1] During a deep sleep, called *hibernation*, animals' body temperatures drop dramatically. [2] How, then, do they maintain homeostasis? [3] Biologists now understand that by lowering their body temperatures, these animals decrease their need for food. [4] The rate at which they burn energy drops. [5] To make this possible, the animals' systems slow down: heart rate drops, breathing slows, and brain activity gets sluggish. [6] In fact, if a predator finds the animal during hibernation, the hibernator is in jeopardy. [7] The animal cannot become alert quickly enough to flee.

[8] Hibernation is not a fool-proof method of making it through winter alive. [9] Animals must either eat enough in late summer and autumn to develop layers of fat to live on as they sleep, or stockpile food where they hibernate so that they can awaken randomly to eat. [10] If the animal is unsuccessful, then it may fall asleep and never wake up to see another spring.

Strategy — Look for clues to word relationships as you read. Look for synonyms and antonyms, in particular.

Test Tip — A synonym of a less familiar word expands your understanding of that word. An antonym helps you understand a less familiar word by stating what it does *not* mean.

1. What information about hibernation would you likely find in a thesaurus?
  - ● Other terms for *hibernation* include *torpor* and *brumation*.
  - Ⓑ Some biologists think that bears hibernate but others do not.
  - Ⓒ The word *hibernate* has, as its root, the Latin word for winter: *hiber*.
  - Ⓓ Some fish and reptiles also spend time in a state similar to hibernation.

2. Which three facts from the passage support the claim in sentence 8 that hibernation is not a "fool-proof" way to survive a long winter?
  - ● A stockpile of food may run out before spring arrives.
  - ● An animal may fail to eat enough food before hibernating.
  - Ⓒ An animal's body temperature may remain too high for it to sleep deeply.
  - ● A predator may find a hibernating animal and kill it before it can wake up.

3. Write the meaning of the word *hibernation*.

  Possible Answer: A deep sleep using a lowered body temperature.

  Why do animals hibernate?

  Possible Answer: Hibernation uses less energy because the body temperature is lower and because animals don't eat as much food.

Spectrum Test Prep Grade 5

English Language Arts
39

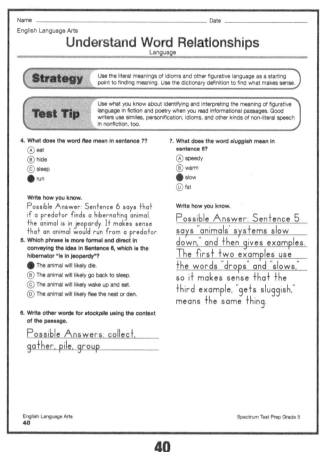

Page 40

Name _____ Date _____

English Language Arts

Understand Word Relationships
Language

Strategy — Use the literal meanings of idioms and other figurative language as a starting point to finding meaning. Use the dictionary definition to find what makes sense.

Test Tip — Use what you know about identifying and interpreting the meaning of figurative language in fiction and poetry when you read informational passages. Good writers use similes, personification, idioms, and other kinds of non-literal speech in nonfiction, too.

4. What does the word *flee* mean in sentence 7?
  - Ⓐ eat
  - Ⓑ hide
  - Ⓒ sleep
  - ● run

5. Which phrase is more formal and direct in conveying the idea in sentence 6, which is the hibernator "is in jeopardy"?
  - ● The animal will likely die.
  - Ⓑ The animal will likely go back to sleep.
  - Ⓒ The animal will likely wake up and eat.
  - Ⓓ The animal will likely flee the nest or den.

6. Write other words for *stockpile* using the context of the passage.

  Possible Answers: collect, gather, pile, group

7. What does the word *sluggish* mean in sentence 5?
  - Ⓐ speedy
  - Ⓑ warm
  - ● slow
  - Ⓤ fat

Write how you know.

Possible Answer: Sentence 6 says that if a predator finds a hibernating animal, the animal is in jeopardy. It makes sense that an animal would run from a predator.

Write how you know.

Possible Answer: Sentence 5 says "animals' systems slow down," and then gives examples. The first two examples use the words "drops" and "slows," so it makes sense that the third example, "gets sluggish," means the same thing.

English Language Arts
40

Spectrum Test Prep Grade 5

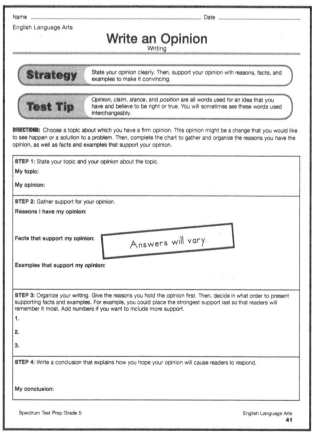

Page 41

Name _____ Date _____

English Language Arts

Write an Opinion
Writing

Strategy — State your opinion clearly. Then, support your opinion with reasons, facts, and examples to make it convincing.

Test Tip — *Opinion*, *claim*, *stance*, and *position* are all words used for an idea that you have and believe to be right or true. You will sometimes see these words used interchangeably.

DIRECTIONS: Choose a topic about which you have a firm opinion. This opinion might be a change that you would like to see happen or a solution to a problem. Then, complete the chart to gather and organize the reasons you have the opinion, as well as facts and examples that support them.

STEP 1: State your topic and your opinion about the topic.

My topic:

My opinion:

STEP 2: Gather support for your opinion.

Reasons I have my opinion:

Facts that support my opinion:

> Answers will vary.

Examples that support my opinion:

STEP 3: Organize your writing. Give the reasons you hold the opinion first. Then, decide in what order to present supporting facts and examples. For example, you could place the strongest support last so that readers will remember it most. Add numbers if you want to include more support.

1.

2.

3.

STEP 4: Write a conclusion that explains how you hope your opinion will cause readers to respond.

My conclusion:

Spectrum Test Prep Grade 5

English Language Arts
41

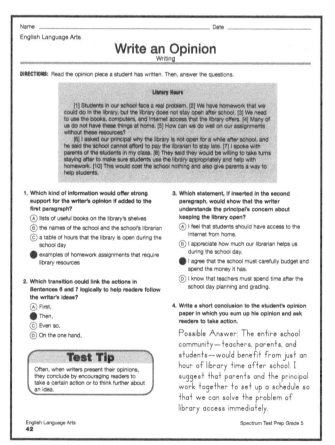

Page 42

Name _____ Date _____

English Language Arts

Write an Opinion
Writing

DIRECTIONS: Read the opinion piece a student has written. Then, answer the questions.

Library Hours

[1] Students in our school face a real problem. [2] We have homework that we could do in the library, but the library does not stay open after school. [3] We need to use the books, computers, and Internet access that the library offers. [4] Many of us do not have these things at home. [5] How can we do well on our assignments without these resources?

[6] I asked our principal why the library is not open for a while after school, and he said the school cannot afford to pay the librarian to stay late. [7] I spoke with parents of the students in my class. [8] They said they would be willing to take turns staying after to make sure the library used the library appropriately and help with homework. [9] This would cost the school nothing and also give parents a way to help students.

1. Which kind of information would offer strong support for the writer's opinion if added to the first paragraph?
  - Ⓐ lists of useful books on the library's shelves
  - Ⓑ the names of the school and the school's librarian
  - Ⓒ a table of hours that the library is open during the school day
  - ● examples of homework assignments that require library resources

2. Which transition could link the actions in Sentences 6 and 7 logically to help readers follow the writer's ideas?
  - Ⓐ First,
  - ● Then,
  - Ⓒ Even so,
  - Ⓓ On the one hand,

Test Tip — Often, when writers present their opinions, they conclude by encouraging readers to take a certain action or to think further about an idea.

3. Which statement, if inserted in the second paragraph, would show that the writer understands the principal's concern about keeping the library open?
  - Ⓐ I feel that students should have access to the Internet from home.
  - Ⓑ I appreciate how much our librarian helps us during the school day.
  - ● I agree that the school must carefully budget and spend the money it has.
  - Ⓓ I know that teachers must spend time after the school day planning and grading.

4. Write a short conclusion to the student's opinion paper in which you sum up his opinion and ask readers to take action.

  Possible Answer: The entire school community—teachers, parents, and students—would benefit from just an hour of library time after school. I suggest that parents and the principal work together to set up a schedule so that we can solve the problem of library access immediately.

English Language Arts
42

Spectrum Test Prep Grade 5

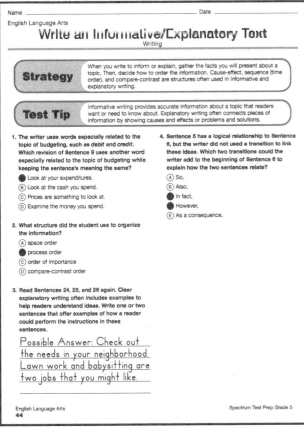

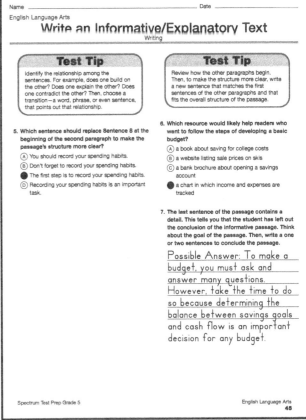

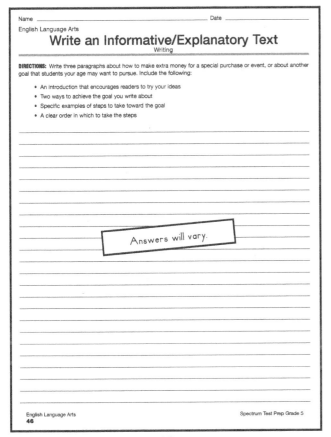

Write a Narrative
Writing

4. Sentences 8 and 9 describe the Peoples' reaction to Grandmother Spider's offer. Write a line or two of dialogue that Opossum might say to explain why the Peoples laugh.
Possible Answer: "Many brave, strong animals have failed to get fire," Opossum said, "but a silly, weak spider thinks she can succeed!"

5. This legend has a beginning that explains the problem—the cold, dark night. It has a middle that develops the problem—no animal is able to get the fire. The legend is missing an end that resolves the problem. Write an ending, based on the events so far, that shows how the problem is solved.
Possible Answer: Many nights later, Grandmother Spider arrived among her people, shivering together in the dark. "Fire!" she cried. "I have it, so bring wood quickly." The Peoples piled wood and watched, amazed and delighted, as Grandmother Spider lit the first fire they had ever seen. No one laughed at the tiny hero now!

DIRECTIONS: A narrative is a story that tells about real or imagined events. Write a narrative about the origin or beginning of something, such as an element in nature. It can be real or imagined. Write your paragraph on the lines. Your paragraph should have the following:
* A narrator and/or characters
* A natural sequence of events
* Dialogue
* Descriptions of actions, thoughts, and feelings
* Time words and phrases to show the order of events
* Concrete words and sensory details
* A sentence to end your paragraph

Strategy
Plan a narrative by choosing people, places, and events that will be in the story. Use an outline or other to keep your ideas organized and to make sure you have details.

Test Tip
Choosing the right words makes a narrative more interesting to read. Use exact words and phrases and figurative language.

Answers will vary.

48

Understand Editing and Revising
Writing

DIRECTIONS: Read the report. Then, answer the questions.

Citizens Protest Tree Removal

[1] Planning for the new community center came to a sudden stop because of a tree. [2] A 60-year-old magnolia tree, to be exact. [3] For years, this tree provided shade for parents who brought their children to swim at the city pool. [4] Since the pool was closed and the new pool opened across town, parents have taken their children to that pool. [5] Now, the magnolia is "in the way" of the new community center, and city planners will announce their plans to cut it down.

[6] But, what they didn't expect was an outcry from citizens. [7] "This tree was a sapling when my grandmother was a girl in this city," said one citizen. [8] I refuse to let these people cut it down, just to make room for some new building! [9] [10] Another protester said, "This tree is healthy. [11] It could live another 40 years. [12] Why chop down such a beautiful magnolia?"

[13] The city planners are taking the citizens' concerns seriously; they are considering building a courtyard around the tree. [14] The magnolia is the state tree of Mississippi and bears large flowers with a strong, sweet odor.

Strategy
When you read to revise, make sure each paragraph of an informative passage has just one main idea. Find and remove details and examples that don't support the main idea.

Test Tip
Revise to clarify your ideas and ensure your reader can understand your meaning.

1. Which sentence in the first paragraph strays from the report's topic and should be removed?
(A) Sentence 2
(B) Sentence 3
● Sentence 4
(D) Sentence 5

Write how you know.
Possible answer: This paragraph talks about the pool being opened across town. This has nothing to do with the paragraph's topic, a tree.

2. Which three revisions to the third paragraph would strengthen the report's conclusion?
(A) Add an explanation about why the city pool had to be moved.
(B) Add a new sentence with instructions on how to care for magnolias.
● Include a quotation from a city planner responding to the citizens' concerns.
● Add a description of what the courtyard might look like.
● Remove the second sentence because it strays from the main idea.

49

Understand Editing and Revising
Writing

3. Which correction should be made so that the tense of Sentence 5 is correct?
(A) Change "is" to "was"
(B) Change "is" to "has been"
● Change "will announce" to "have announced"
(D) Change "will announce" to "will have announced"

Write how you know.
The tense of the sentence should be past tense so it matches the rest of the report.

4. What change is needed so that Sentence 8 is correctly punctuated?
(A) Add a comma after "people."
● Place the sentence in quotation marks.
(C) Change the comma after "down" to a period.
(D) Change the exclamation point to a question mark.

Write how you know.
The sentence should be in quotation marks because it is dialogue.

Test Tip
Revise to ensure that each sentence expresses a complete thought. Identify sentence fragments by checking that each sentence has a subject and verb that agree. If a sentence is missing either the subject or the verb, it is a fragment and should be revised.

5. Sentence 2 is a fragment. It has a subject but no verb that agrees with the subject. Revise sentence 2 either by writing it as a complete sentence or by combining it with another sentence.
Possible Answers: The tree in question is a 60-year-old magnolia tree. Planning for the new community center has come to a sudden stop because of a 60-year-old magnolia tree. For years, this 60-year-old magnolia tree provided shade for parents who brought their children to swim at the city pool.

50

Strategy Review

1. Review "Cheerful Crawfish." Then, state a theme of the passage in your own words. Give a detail that supports the theme of the passage.
Possible Answer: Don't give up if the first attempt fails. If you keep trying, you may achieve your goal after all. Dove's attempt fails to produce results, but Crawfish was able to find land.

Strategy
Identify literary or structural elements and use them to understand the meaning of a text.

A *genre* is a type of literature, such as poetry, drama, or legend. If you can identify the genre of what you read, you can interpret what you read more easily.

2. How can you tell that "Cheerful Crawfish" is a legend or myth? Choose three answers.
● Animals talk and reason.
● Magical or unreal events happen.
● The story is set "before the beginning."
(D) The characters learn an important lesson.
(E) The story has a beginning, middle, and end.

Strategy
Reread texts to make comparisons, draw conclusions, or support inferences.

My hand is to me what your hearing and sight together are to you. In large measure we travel the same highways, read the same books, speak the same language, yet our experiences are different. All my comings and goings turn on the hand as on a pivot. It is the hand that binds me to the world of men and women. . . . With the dropping of a little word from another's hand into mine, a slight flutter of the fingers, began the intelligence, the joy, the fullness of my very life.

—Helen Keller, from *The World I Live In*

A childhood illness left Helen Keller deaf and blind, without the means to communicate with others. Her teacher, Annie Sullivan, helped her learn to communicate again by spelling words into her hand. Keller developed a deep love of language and became a writer, an adventurous outdoorswoman and avid boater, and a well-known American citizen around the world. She attended college with her teacher by her side, experienced art by touching art works, and even sensed music through the vibrations of instruments.

3. Part A: What can readers infer about Keller, based on her words and the passage?
(A) She did not care for art or music.
● She was not afraid to learn new things.
(C) She could communicate only through her teacher.
(D) She remained sad about losing her ability to see and hear.

Part B: Cite a detail from the excerpt that supports your answer to Part A.
Possible answer: She participated in outdoor activities, including on the water, even though she could not see.

52

Strategy Review

Strategy
Use word clues in a text to identify its structure, to see how ideas in a text are related, and to clarify word meanings.

Foley artists create the sound effects for television shows and for movies—the creaks, bangs, footsteps, slamming doors, and so on. Many people think that film sounds are simply recorded as the actors play the scenes. However, sets are not real places, and so the sounds made in sets don't sound real. For instance, a floor that looks like stone might really be painted wood, so footsteps on the floor sound like footsteps on wood. Foley artists replace the "wrong" footsteps with the "right" sound effect. Because sounds on film are usually a mix of recorded sounds, Foley artists experiment with combinations to give the world of film verity. That is, they make the world of film sound like viewers expect it to sound.

Transitions are words or phrases that show how ideas are connected. Words like *before, following,* or *next* can signal how events are related in time. Transitions like *because* or *so* can show a cause-effect relationship. Other transitions, such as *but* and *however,* signal contrast. Use the Internet to find lists of more transitions.

1. Write a phrase from the passage that tells readers an example is coming up.

For instance

Context clues are words or phrases within a passage that help you understand unfamiliar words. Sometimes, the writer will make the definition obvious by using phrases that rename, describe, or give examples of the unfamiliar word. Look at the sentences before and after the unfamiliar word to find context clues.

2. Write the phrase from the passage that helps you find the meaning of the word *verity*.

"they make the world of film sound like viewers expect it to sound."

Spectrum Test Prep Grade 5

English Language Arts
53

53

Strategy Review

Strategy When writing, use details to support, explain, or clarify your main ideas.

[1] Biomimicry: the word combines *bio-*, meaning life, and *mimic*, meaning to imitate. [2] Engineers use biomimicry to build useful things based on nature. [3] Velcro, for example, is a very useful material. [4] It was inspired by tiny hooks on burrs. [5] I once had shoes that closed with Velcro rather than laces. [6] Chemists are studying lotus flower petals to understand how they stay perfectly clean even when growing in mud. [7] The chemists hope to develop paints that shed dirt, based on the design of the petals. [8] Nature offers inspiration for how to go fast, how to stay cold, and how to catch water. [9] These living, growing things are teaching people how to solve problems and meet needs.

Details can be either helpful or distracting. The writer of this passage knows that some readers will not know much about biomimicry. So, she provides several details to explain biomimicry. Examples, descriptions, and explanations of processes help, too. However, adding details that don't relate to the main idea may confuse readers.

1. Which sentence in the passage presents a detail that does not relate to the main idea?
   (A) Sentence 1
   (B) Sentence 3
   ● Sentence 5
   (D) Sentence 8

When you have a writing assignment and not much time to plan, a scratch outline can help you quickly pull together ideas. These outlines get their name from the way they're written—very quickly and informally, maybe even scratched on a piece of scratch paper. A quick look at this outline shows that the writer has not gathered all the information needed for the opinion essay.

Scratch Outline for Opinion Essay
STEP 1: State your topic and your opinion about the topic.
My topic: *homework*
My opinion: *Students should have at least thirty minutes of homework each evening.*

Support for my opinion:	Objections to my opinion:
1. *There is not enough class time to practice skills.*	1. Many students are involved in sports or music activities after school.
2. *Reviewing skills soon after learning them help students master them.*	2.
3.	3. Students would rather play than do homework.

Conclusion: *Thirty minutes of homework each evening is enough to help students review and retain what they learned during the school day.*

2. Based on the outline, what does the writer need to do before drafting his opinion on homework requirements?

Possible Answer: The writer needs to spend time thinking about what other problems might arise if students had homework every night. The writer also needs more reasons that support the opinion that setting time aside to do homework is the right thing to do.

English Language Arts
54

Spectrum Test Prep Grade 5

54

Strategy Review

Strategy Use transitions to show how ideas are related.

If you're going to go to the trouble to paint a room, do it right—the first time. To begin, clean the wall and trim carefully, and let it dry. _____, patch any little holes in the wall. You can get a patch kit at any home improvement store. Then, cover all furniture and carpets with drop cloths in case you spill paint. (You probably will spill a little.) Gather your tools—brushes, rags, and rollers. Now you are ready, _____, to open the paint can and prepare to add a new color to your world.

When you need to describe a series of events, you can do so to tell readers how to do something, or you can do so to explain why things happen as they do. Use time transitions words such as *first, next,* and *finally* to show how events are related in time. Use cause-effect transitions such as *because* and *consequently* to show how causes and effects are related.

1. Write transitions that connect the steps in the painting process. Make sure each transition connects the ideas in a way that makes sense.

Next _____ at last

Strategy
Revise to make sure your writing is clear and makes sense. Then, edit to fix errors.

Writing is more interesting when it is clear. To make writing clear, think about how readers perceive the world. We use all our senses—sight, hearing, touch, taste, smell—to relate to the world. Even temperature and texture help us experience the world. Writers work to include sense details in their stories, to bring the stories to life. Here's how one writer described a storm approaching:

The smell of rain was in the heavy air, even though the thunder was still distant and muted. Sudden breezes gusted, scattering dry leaves this way and that and sending a message that the rain would soon arrive.

2. Write another sentence that includes sense details to describe how people might perceive the coming storm.

Possible Answer: The day had been warm and sticky, but as the clouds rolled closer, the air became cool, crisp, and refreshing—a welcome change.

3. Which of the following sentences contains incorrect punctuation?
   ● Glancing at the darkening sky; Kate worried.
   (B) If the storm broke, the picnic would be ruined.
   (C) Thundered rumbled, but it was still far away.
   (D) The picnic was ready to serve: sandwiches, fruit, and bottles of water.

Spectrum Test Prep Grade 5

English Language Arts
55

55

Evaluate Numerical Expressions
Operations and Algebraic Thinking

DIRECTIONS: Choose or write the correct answer.

Strategy When evaluating expressions, use the order of operations **PEMDAS**: Parentheses, Exponents, Multiply or Divide before Add or Subtract.

1. The expression below represents the number of students at Luisa's school who helped at the school fair. How many students helped at the school fair?

$4 \times [33 - 3 \times (5 + 2)]$

   (A) 840
   (B) 208
   (C) 80
   ● 48

2. Which expressions have a value of 8? Choose all that apply.
   ● $12 \times (4 + 2) \div 9$
   (B) $(4 \times 2) + (8 \div 0) + 8$
   ● $36 \div 9 + [(4 \times 5) \div 5]$
   ● $[5 (10 - 8) + 4] - 2 \times 3$
   (E) $(4 + 12 \div 3) + [12 - 3 \times (4 - 2)]$

3. Which two expressions have the same value as the expression below?

$2\{10 \times [(33 + 25) - 25]\}$

   ● $10 \times (55 + 11) - 50 \times 2 + (200 \div 2)$
   ● $\{[3 \times 20 + 5 \times 20 + 2,000 \div 2] - 10 \times 50\}$
   (C) $138 + \{550 - [6 + (25 - 10 \div 5)]\}$
   (D) $120 + (160 \times 4 \div 2) + 6 \times 20$
   (E) $\{120 + [2 + (400 - 200) \times 2] - 20$

4. Evaluate the expression $44 \times (9 + 3) \div 2$. Show your work.

264:
$44 \times (12) \div 2 = 44 \times 6 = 264$

5. Jake wrote the expression below to represent the number of minutes he practiced playing the guitar during the week. Evaluate the expression to show how long he practiced. Show your work.

$5 \times 30 + 2 \times (30 + 15)$

240:
$5 \times 30 + 2 \times (30 + 15) =$
$5 \times 30 + 2 \times 45 =$
$150 + 90 = 240$

Spectrum Test Prep Grade 5

Math
57

57

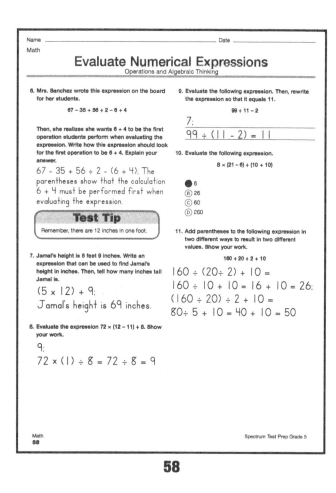

Evaluate Numerical Expressions
Operations and Algebraic Thinking

6. Mrs. Sanchez wrote this expression on the board for her students.

67 − 35 + 56 ÷ 2 − 6 + 4

Then, she realizes she wants 6 + 4 to be the first operation students perform when evaluating the expression. Write how this expression should look for the first operation to be 6 + 4. Explain your answer.

67 − 35 + 56 ÷ 2 − (6 + 4); The parentheses show that the calculation 6 + 4 must be performed first when evaluating the expression.

Test Tip
Remember, there are 12 inches in one foot.

7. Jamal's height is 5 feet 9 inches. Write an expression that can be used to find Jamal's height in inches. Then, tell how many inches tall Jamal is.

(5 × 12) + 9; Jamal's height is 69 inches.

8. Evaluate the expression 72 × (12 − 11) ÷ 8. Show your work.

9; 72 × (1) ÷ 8 = 72 ÷ 8 = 9

9. Evaluate the following expression. Then, rewrite the expression so that it equals 11.

99 ÷ 11 − 2

7; 99 ÷ (11 − 9) = 11

10. Evaluate the following expression.

8 × (21 − 6) ÷ (10 + 10)

● 6
Ⓑ 26
Ⓒ 60
Ⓓ 260

11. Add parentheses to the following expression in two different ways to result in two different values. Show your work.

160 ÷ 20 ÷ 2 + 10

160 ÷ (20 ÷ 2) + 10 = 160 ÷ 10 + 10 = 16 + 10 = 26; (160 ÷ 20) ÷ 2 + 10 = 80 ÷ 5 + 10 = 40 + 10 = 50

58

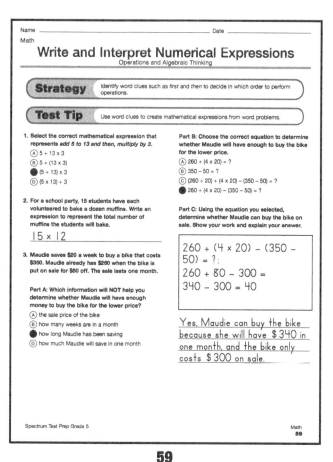

Write and Interpret Numerical Expressions
Operations and Algebraic Thinking

Strategy Identify word clues such as *first* and *then* to decide in which order to perform operations.

Test Tip Use word clues to create mathematical expressions from word problems.

1. Select the correct mathematical expression that represents *add 5 to 13 and then, multiply by 3*.
Ⓐ 5 + 13 × 3
Ⓑ 5 + (13 × 3)
● (5 + 13) × 3
Ⓓ (5 × 13) + 3

2. For a school party, 15 students have each volunteered to bake a dozen muffins. Write an expression to represent the total number of muffins the students will bake.

15 × 12

3. Maudie saves $20 a week to buy a bike that costs $350. Maudie already has $260 when the bike is put on sale for $50 off. The sale lasts one month.

Part A: Which information will NOT help you determine whether Maudie will have enough money to buy the bike for the lower price?
Ⓐ the sale price of the bike
Ⓑ how many weeks are in a month
● how long Maudie has been saving
Ⓓ how much Maudie will save in one month

Part B: Choose the correct equation to determine whether Maudie will have enough to buy the bike for the lower price.
Ⓐ 260 + (4 × 20) = ?
Ⓑ 350 − 50 = ?
Ⓒ (260 ÷ 20) + (4 × 20) − (350 − 50) = ?
● 260 + (4 × 20) − (350 − 50) = ?

Part C: Using the equation you selected, determine whether Maudie can buy the bike on sale. Show your work and explain your answer.

260 + (4 × 20) − (350 − 50) = ?; 260 + 80 − 300 = 340 − 300 = 40

Yes, Maudie can buy the bike because she will have $340 in one month, and the bike only costs $300 on sale.

59

Write and Interpret Numerical Expressions
Operations and Algebraic Thinking

Strategy When comparing mathematical expressions, first identify terms that are the same. Then, identify how they are different.

4. Compare the following mathematical expressions and indicate whether each statement is true or false.

A: 2 × (423 + 20,789)   B: 4 × (423 + 20,789)

The value of A is two times the value of B.	true	(false)
The value of B is two times the value of A.	(true)	false
A + A = B	(true)	false
B − A = A	(true)	false
B + A = A + A	true	(false)

5. Compare the following mathematical expressions and choose the correct statement.

A: (2 × 4) × (4 + 25)   B: (2 × 8) × (4 + 25)

Ⓐ The value of A is equal to the value of B.
Ⓑ The value of B is equal to the value of A.
Ⓒ The value of A is twice the value of B.
● The value of A is half the value of B.

6. Three 6th grade classes are making flags for a school project. Each class will need 20 yards of blue fabric, 10 yards of red fabric, and 5 yards of yellow ribbon. If the amount of materials needed for one class is represented as 20b + 10r + 5y, choose all the expressions that represent the total amount of materials needed for all three classes.

● 60b + 30r + 15y
Ⓑ (3 × 20b) + 10r + 5y
Ⓒ 3 × (20b + 10r + 5y)
Ⓓ 30b + 30r + 30y

7. Jessie is making bracelets for a fundraiser. Each bracelet will use 30 green beads, 6 black beads, and 12 silver beads. Write an expression that Jessie can use to find the total number of beads needed to make 25 bracelets. Then, find the amount of money Jessie will need to buy the beads if each bead costs $0.20. Show your work.

25(30 + 6 + 12); 25(30 + 6 + 12) = 1,200; 1,200 × $0.25 = $240.00

60

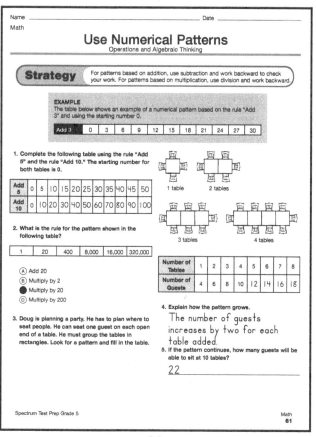

Use Numerical Patterns
Operations and Algebraic Thinking

Strategy For patterns based on addition, use subtraction and work backward to check your work. For patterns based on multiplication, use division and work backward.

EXAMPLE
The table below shows an example of a numerical pattern based on the rule "Add 3" and using the starting number 0.

Add 3	0	3	6	9	12	15	18	21	24	27	30

1. Complete the following table using the rule "Add 5" and the rule "Add 10." The starting number for both tables is 0.

Add 5	0	5	10	15	20	25	30	35	40	45	50
Add 10	0	10	20	30	40	50	60	70	80	90	100

2. What is the rule for the pattern shown in the following table?

1	20	400	8,000	16,000	320,000

Ⓐ Add 20
Ⓑ Multiply by 2
● Multiply by 20
Ⓓ Multiply by 200

3. Doug is planning a party. He has to plan where to seat people. He can seat one guest on each open end of a table. He must group the tables in rectangles. Look for a pattern and fill in the table.

Number of Tables	1	2	3	4	5	6	7	8
Number of Guests	4	6	8	10	12	14	16	18

4. Explain how the pattern grows.

The number of guests increases by two for each table added.

5. If the pattern continues, how many guests will be able to sit at 10 tables?

22

61

Name _____ Date _____
Math

Graph Ordered Pairs
Operations and Algebraic Thinking

Strategy Use a coordinate plane to graph ordered pairs of numbers. Use your graph to answer questions.

Test Tip A plane must travel along the ground before it takes off. So, when graphing, move left to right along the x-axis first; then, move up or down.

1. Complete the following table using the rule "Add 2" and the rule "Add 4."

Add 2	0	2	4	6	8	10
Add 4	0	4	8	12	16	20

Form ordered pairs from the two patterns.

(0, 0) (2, 4) (4, _8_) (_6_, _12_)

(8, _16_) (10, 20)

Graph the ordered pairs

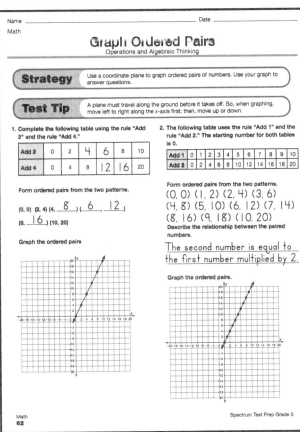

2. The following table uses the rule "Add 1" and the rule "Add 2." The starting number for both tables is 0.

Add 1	0	1	2	3	4	5	6	7	8	9	10
Add 2	0	2	4	6	8	10	12	14	16	18	20

Form ordered pairs from the two patterns.

(0, 0) (1, 2) (2, 4) (3, 6)
(4, 8) (5, 10) (6, 12) (7, 14)
(8, 16) (9, 18) (10, 20)

Describe the relationship between the paired numbers.

The second number is equal to the first number multiplied by 2.

Graph the ordered pairs.

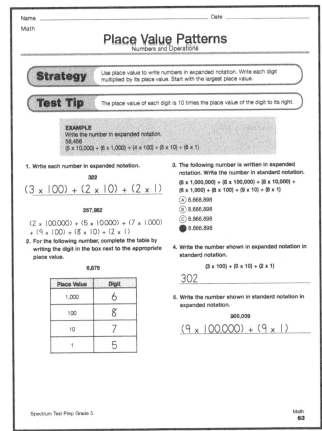

Spectrum Test Prep Grade 5

Name _____ Date _____
Math

Place Value Patterns
Numbers and Operations

Strategy Use place value to write numbers in expanded notation. Write each digit multiplied by its place value. Start with the largest place value.

Test Tip The place value of each digit is 10 times the place value of the digit to its right.

EXAMPLE
Write the number in expanded notation.
58,456
(5 x 10,000) + (6 x 1,000) + (4 x 100) + (5 x 10) + (6 x 1)

1. Write each number in expanded notation.

322

(3 x 100) + (2 x 10) + (2 x 1)

257,982

(2 x 100,000) + (5 x 10,000) + (7 x 1,000) + (9 x 100) + (8 x 10) + (2 x 1)

2. For the following number, complete the table by writing the digit in the box next to the appropriate place value.

6,875

Place Value	Digit
1,000	6
100	8
10	7
1	5

3. The following number is written in expanded notation. Write the number in standard notation.

(8 x 1,000,000) + (8 x 100,000) + (8 x 10,000) + (6 x 1,000) + (8 x 100) + (9 x 10) + (8 x 1)

Ⓐ 8,668,898
Ⓑ 8,686,898
Ⓒ 8,866,898
● 8,886,898

4. Write the number shown in expanded notation in standard notation.

(3 x 100) + (0 x 10) + (2 x 1)

302

5. Write the number shown in standard notation in expanded notation.

900,009

(9 x 100,000) + (9 x 1)

Name _____ Date _____
Math

Place Value Patterns
Numbers and Operations

Strategy Create a table to use place value in multi-digit numbers. Write each digit in its correct place value: thousandths, hundreds, tens, ones.

Test Tip In a multi-digit number, the place value of each digit is $\frac{1}{10}$ times the place value of the digit to its left.

EXAMPLE
The following number is written in expanded notation.
(4 x $\frac{1}{10}$) + (5 x $\frac{1}{100}$) + (6 x $\frac{1}{1000}$)
This is the same number written in standard notation: 0.456

6. The following number is written in expanded notation.

(3 x 10) + (2 x 1) + (2 x $\frac{1}{10}$) + (3 x $\frac{1}{100}$)

Which number in standard notation is equivalent?
Ⓐ 0.0799
Ⓑ 322.3
● 32.23
Ⓓ 23.23

7. The following number is written in standard notation. Write the number in expanded form.

0.45

(4 x $\frac{1}{10}$) + (5 x $\frac{1}{100}$)

8. The following number is written in expanded notation.

(7 x $\frac{1}{10}$) + (9 x $\frac{1}{100}$) + (9 x $\frac{1}{1000}$)

Which number in standard notation is equivalent?
Ⓐ 0.0799
● 0.799
Ⓒ 7.99
Ⓓ 79.9

9. The following number is written in expanded notation.

(8 x 1000) + (7 x 100) + (2 x 10) + (9 x 1) + (5 x $\frac{1}{10}$) + (5 x $\frac{1}{100}$)

Write the number in standard notation.

8,729.55

Spectrum Test Prep Grade 5

Name _____ Date _____
Math

Powers of 10
Numbers and Operations

Strategy Use exponents to convert the power of 10 to standard notation. Then, use the standard notation number in your calculations.

Test Tip Read all parts of the question first.

1. The following numbers are expressed as multiples of powers of 10. Write the numbers as whole numbers in standard notation.

(6 x 10^1) = (6 x 10) =

60

(8 x 10^3) = (8 x 1,000) =

8,000

2. The table below shows powers of 10 for whole numbers.

10^0	10^1	10^2	10^3	10^4	10^5
1	10	100	1,000	10,000	100,000

Complete the table below for additional powers of 10.

10^6	10^7	10^8	10^9
1,000,000	10,000,000	100,000,000	1,000,000,000

Test Tip
When multiplying by powers of 10, use this pattern to check your work and make sure your answer has the correct number of digits.

3. Explain the relationship between the power of 10 and the number of zeroes in the corresponding number. Give an example.

The number that shows the power of 10 also tells how many zeroes are in the number. For example, 10^2 = 100, which has two zeroes.

4. Write the following numbers as multiples of powers of 10.

90,000

(9 x 10^4)

4

(4 x 10^0)

700

(7 x 10^2)

5. The following number is expressed in expanded notation. Write the number as multiples of powers of 10 and in standard notation.

(3 x 1000) + (2 x 100) + (6 x 10)

(3 x 10^3) + (2 x 10^2) + (6 x 10^1);
3,260

Powers of 10
Numbers and Operations

DIRECTIONS: Multiply or divide by powers of 10. Write the answers as whole numbers or decimals.

Strategy Check your work by reading it in words.
For example, 25 ÷ 1,000 = 0.025 can be read as "twenty-five divided by one thousand equals twenty-five thousandths."

6. $9 \div 10^0 = 9 \div 1 = $ __9__

7. $20 \div 10^3 = 20 \div 1,000 = $ __0.02__

8. $0.5 \times$ __10^1__ $= 5$

9. $6 \div$ __10^2__ $= 0.06$

10. $9 \div$ __1,000__ $= 0.009$

11. $0.6 \times$ __10^4__ $= 6,000$

12. **Part A:** Dani and Marcus are measuring distances in the lab. They record some of the distances in centimeters and others in meters. They know that 1 meter = 100 centimeters, so they decide to use powers of 10 to convert all their measurements to meters so they can compare distances. Their results are shown in the table below.

Measurement in centimeters (A)	Measurement in meters (B)
45	0.45
203	2.03
97	0.97
3.5	0.035

What is the correct equation for converting centimeters to meters?
- Ⓐ $A \times 10^2 = B$
- ● $A \div 10^2 = B$
- Ⓒ $A \times 10^3 = B$
- Ⓓ $A \div 10^3 = B$

Part B: Dani and Marcus begin to notice a pattern and realize they can convert their measurements without performing a calculation each time. Choose all that describe the pattern they discover.
- Ⓐ To convert centimeters to meters, move the decimal point two spaces to the right.
- ● To convert meters to centimeters, move the decimal point two spaces to the right.
- Ⓑ 0.846 = ...
- ● To convert centimeters to meters, move the decimal point two spaces to the left.
- Ⓓ To convert meters to centimeters, move the decimal point two spaces to the left.

66

Read and Write Decimals
Numbers and Operations

Strategy Use place value to the right of the decimal point to write decimals in expanded form.

1. Write the following numbers in expanded form.
5.642
$$(5 \times 1) + (6 \times \tfrac{1}{10}) + (4 \times \tfrac{1}{100}) + (2 \times \tfrac{1}{1000})$$

2. **4,257.21**
$$(4 \times 1,000) + (2 \times 100) + (5 \times 10) + (7 \times 1) + (2 \times \tfrac{1}{10}) + (1 \times \tfrac{1}{100})$$

3. Choose all the equations that are true.
- ● $22,336.462 = (2 \times 10,000) + (2 \times 1,000) + (3 \times 100) + (3 \times 10) + (6 \times 1) + (4 \times \tfrac{1}{10} + (6 \times \tfrac{1}{100}) + (2 \times \tfrac{1}{1000})$
- Ⓑ $0.846 = (8 \times \tfrac{1}{10}) + (4 \times \tfrac{1}{1000}) + (6 \times \tfrac{1}{10,000})$
- ● $3,047.45 = (3 \times 1,000) + (4 \times 10) + (7 \times 1) + (4 \times \tfrac{1}{10}) + (5 \times \tfrac{1}{100})$
- ● $6.006 = (6 \times 1) + (6 \times \tfrac{1}{1000})$

Strategy When writing numbers in expanded form, start by determining how many terms your answer will have; you should have as many terms as there are digits in the number.

4. Write 2.25 in word form.
__two and twenty-five hundredths__

5. Choose the number that is equivalent to *three thousand forty-five and seven thousandths.*
- ● 3,045.007
- Ⓑ 3,450.007
- Ⓒ 3,450.007
- Ⓓ 3,045.07

6. Write 75,296.999 in word form.
__seventy-five thousand two hundred ninety-six and nine hundred ninety-nine thousandths__

7. Write 3.75 in word form.
__three and seventy-five hundredths__

8. Choose the number that is equivalent to *two thousand fifty-five and six thousandths.*
- Ⓐ 2,550.06
- ● 2,055.006
- Ⓒ 2,550.006
- Ⓓ 2,056.06

67

Compare Decimals
Numbers and Operations

Strategy Use numbers and place value to compare pairs of decimals.

Test Tip Remember that < is read "less than" and > is read "greater than."

1. For each pair of numbers below, use >, =, or < to show whether the first number (A) is greater than, equal to, or less than the second number (B).

A	>, =, <	B
52.16	<	52.17
30.99	=	30.990
200.02	>	200.002
0.123	<	0.223

2. For each pair of numbers below, use >, =, or < to show whether the first number (A) is greater than, equal to, or less than the second number (B).

A	>, =, <	B
99.50	=	99.5000
154.120	>	154.089
5,789.2	<	57,892.8
0.094	>	0.0094

3. Order the following numbers from greatest to least by writing a 1, 2, 3, or 4 in the boxes below.

- [3] $(6 \times \tfrac{1}{100})$
- [2] (2.2×1000)
- [4] $(2 \times \tfrac{1}{1000})$
- [1] (12×1000)

4. Jessie buys two pieces of candy. One weighs one tenth of a pound and the other weighs 94 thousandths of a pound. Jessie tells her brother he can have the larger piece and offers him the first piece. He says the second piece is larger because 94 is greater than 1 and 1000 is greater than 10.

Who is right, Jessie or her brother?
__Jessie__

Explain how you know which piece is larger.
__Possible Answer: If you write the values as numbers, you can see that 0.1 is larger than 0.094. One-tenth is equal to 100 thousandths, which is greater than 94 thousandths.__

68

Round Decimals
Numbers and Operations

DIRECTIONS: Read each question. Choose or write the correct answer.

Strategy Use place value to round decimals. Look at the digit following the place value you are rounding to. If the digit is 5 or higher, round up.

1. Round 536.28 to the nearest tenth.
- Ⓐ 536
- Ⓑ 536.2
- ● 536.3
- Ⓓ 536.29

Test Tip Think of a number line. Ask yourself, *What two numbers is this number between? Which number is it closer to?*

2. Round 100.92 to the nearest whole number.
- Ⓐ 100
- ● 101
- Ⓒ 100.9
- Ⓓ 100.93

3. Round 57.2 to the nearest 10.
- Ⓐ 50
- Ⓑ 57
- Ⓒ 58
- ● 60

4. Round 47.65 to the nearest tenth.
__47.7__

5. Round 850.049 to the nearest 100.
__900__

6. Round 0.075 to the nearest hundredth.
__0.08__

7. Round 1,286.007 to the nearest hundredth.
- Ⓐ 1,286
- Ⓑ 1,286.1
- ● 1,286.01
- Ⓓ 1,286.107

8. Janice is asked to round 0.604 to the nearest whole number on a test. She says the correct answer is 1. Is she correct? If she made a mistake, explain her mistake.
__She is correct.__

9. Barry is asked to round 30.217 to the nearest 10 on a homework assignment. He says the correct answer is 30.22. Is he correct? If he made a mistake, explain his mistake.
__He is incorrect. He rounded the number to the nearest tenth, not the nearest 10. The correct answer is 30.__

69

Round Decimals
Numbers and Operations

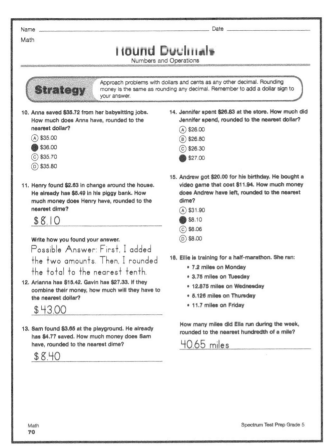

Strategy Approach problems with dollars and cents as any other decimal. Rounding money is the same as rounding any decimal. Remember to add a dollar sign to your answer.

10. Anna saved $35.72 from her babysitting jobs. How much does Anna have, rounded to the nearest dollar?
    - (A) $35.00
    - ● $36.00
    - (C) $35.70
    - (D) $35.80

11. Henry found $2.63 in change around the house. He already has $5.49 in his piggy bank. How much money does Henry have, rounded to the nearest dime?
    $8.10
    Write how you found your answer.
    Possible Answer: First, I added the two amounts. Then, I rounded the total to the nearest tenth.

12. Arianna has $15.42. Gavin has $27.33. If they combine their money, how much will they have to the nearest dollar?
    $43.00

13. Sam found $3.65 at the playground. He already has $4.77 saved. How much money does Sam have, rounded to the nearest dime?
    $8.40

14. Jennifer spent $26.83 at the store. How much did Jennifer spend, rounded to the nearest dollar?
    - (A) $26.00
    - (B) $26.80
    - (C) $26.30
    - ● $27.00

15. Andrew got $20.00 for his birthday. He bought a video game that cost $11.94. How much money does Andrew have left, rounded to the nearest dime?
    - (A) $31.90
    - ● $8.10
    - (C) $8.06
    - (D) $8.00

16. Ellie is training for a half-marathon. She ran:
    - 7.2 miles on Monday
    - 3.75 miles on Tuesday
    - 12.875 miles on Wednesday
    - 5.126 miles on Thursday
    - 11.7 miles on Friday

    How many miles did Ellie run during the week, rounded to the nearest hundredth of a mile?
    40.65 miles

Math
70

Spectrum Test Prep Grade 5

70

Multiply and Divide
Numbers and Operations

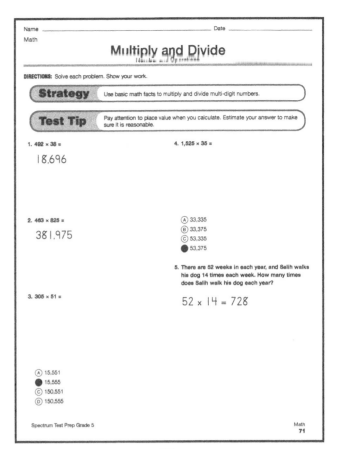

DIRECTIONS: Solve each problem. Show your work.

Strategy Use basic math facts to multiply and divide multi-digit numbers.

Test Tip Pay attention to place value when you calculate. Estimate your answer to make sure it is reasonable.

1. 492 × 38 =
   18,696

2. 463 × 825 =
   381,975

3. 305 × 51 =
   - (A) 15,551
   - ● 15,555
   - (C) 150,551
   - (D) 150,555

4. 1,525 × 35 =
   - (A) 33,335
   - (B) 33,375
   - (C) 53,335
   - ● 53,375

5. There are 52 weeks in each year, and Salih walks his dog 14 times each week. How many times does Salih walk his dog each year?
   52 × 14 = 728

Spectrum Test Prep Grade 5

Math
71

71

Multiply and Divide
Numbers and Operations

DIRECTIONS: Solve each problem. Show your work.

Strategy Identify clue words or operations symbols in word problems to know whether to multiply or divide.

6. 1,728 ÷ 24 =
   72

7. 777 ÷ 7 =
   111

8. 2,185 ÷ 5 =
   - ● 437
   - (B) 447
   - (C) 537
   - (D) 547

9. 4,640 ÷ 32 =
   - (A) 140
   - (B) 145
   - (C) 150
   - (D) 155

10. Martine solved the following division problem: 549 ÷ 9 = 61. Write an equation she could use to estimate and see if her answer is reasonable.
    Possible Answer:
    550 ÷ 10 = 55

11. Nathan checked his work on a problem by estimating using the following equation: 900 ÷ 10 = 90. Write an equation he could have been checking. Give the exact answer to your equation.
    Possible Answer:
    896 ÷ 8 = 112

Math
72

Spectrum Test Prep Grade 5

72

Add and Subtract Decimals
Numbers and Operations

DIRECTIONS: Solve each problem.

Strategy Use adding and subtracting whole numbers to add and subtract decimals.

Test Tip Look carefully at the equation to know which operation to perform. Remember to line up the decimal points.

1. 2.14 + 3.01 = 5.15

2. 18.7 − 12.05 = 6.65

3. Natalie wrote that 773.15 − 200.4 = 2,531. What mistake did she make?
   Possible Answer: Instead of aligning the decimal points, Natalie aligned the last digits.

4. 664.72 + 323.85 =
   - ● 988.57
   - (B) 340.87
   - (C) 987.157
   - (D) 9.8857

5. Chris bought a phone for $250.63. He paid $35.15 for a case. What was the total amount he spent?
   $285.78

6. 1.37 − 0.52 = 0.85

7. Cameron bought a CD for $15.45. He paid $1.16 in tax. What was the total cost of the CD?
   $16.61

8. Julia bought a pair of boots for $45.50. She had a coupon for $10 off and paid $1.78 in sales tax. What was the total cost of the boots? Show your work.
   $45.50 − $10.00 = $35.50;
   $35.50 + $1.78 = $37.28
   total cost

9. Mallory bought a bag of cat food for $15.41. She had a coupon for $5.00 off and paid $1.08 in sales tax. How much did she spend all together? Show your work.
   $15.41 − $5.00 = $10.41;
   $10.41 + $1.08 = she spent
   $11.49 all together

Spectrum Test Prep Grade 5

Math
73

73

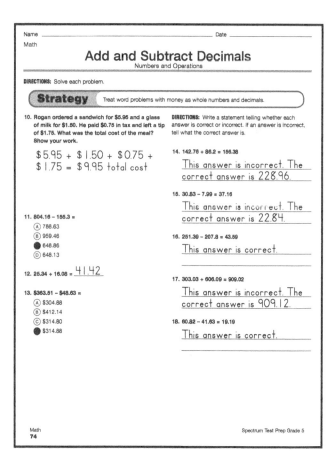

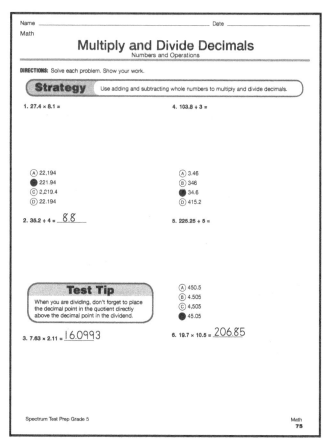

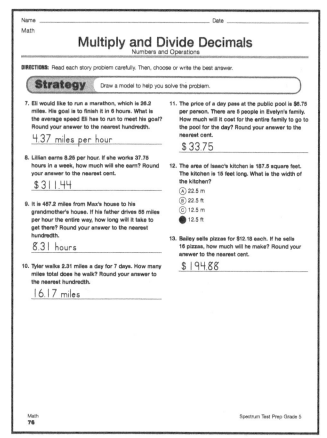

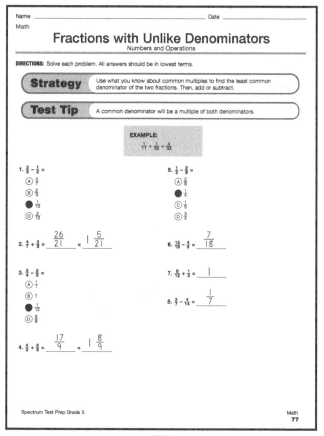

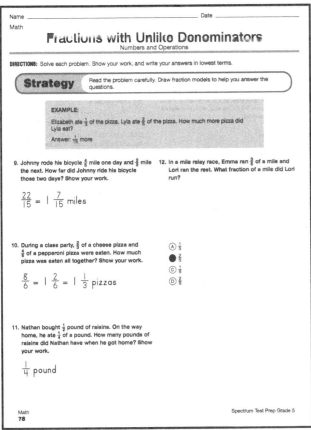

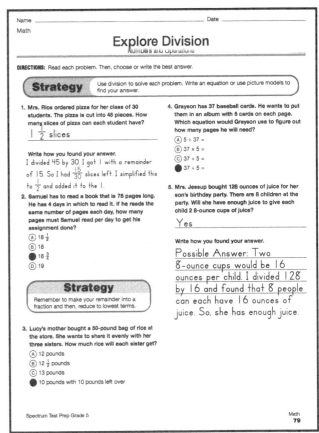

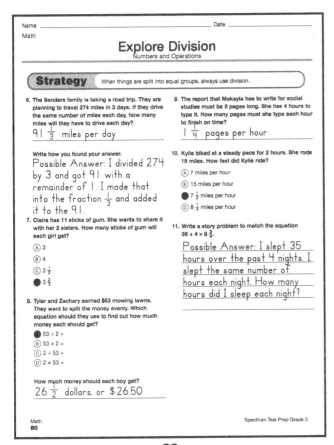

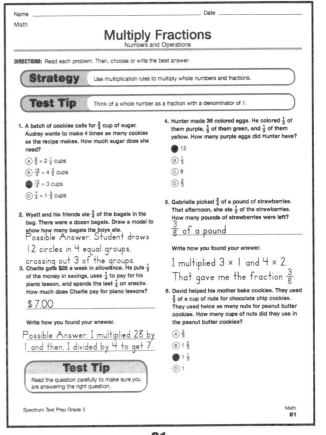

78

79

80

81

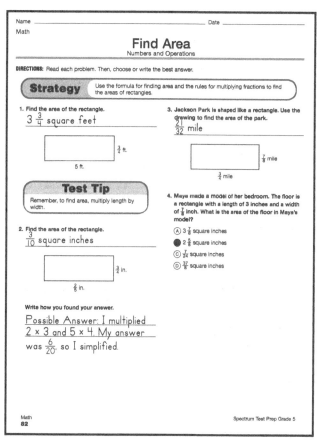

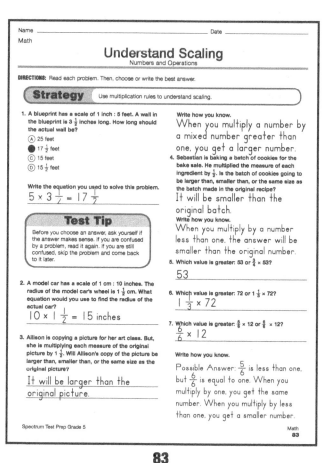

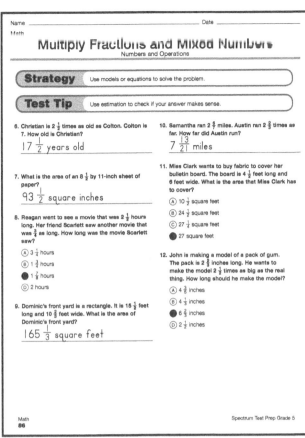

Multiply Fractions and Mixed Numbers
Numbers and Operations

Strategy Use models or equations to solve the problem.

Test Tip Use estimation to check if your answer makes sense.

6. Christian is $2\frac{1}{2}$ times as old as Colton. Colton is 7. How old is Christian?

$17\frac{1}{2}$ years old

7. What is the area of an $8\frac{1}{2}$ by 11-inch sheet of paper?

$93\frac{1}{2}$ square inches

8. Reagan went to see a movie that was $2\frac{1}{2}$ hours long. Her friend Scarlett saw another movie that was $\frac{3}{4}$ as long. How long was the movie Scarlett saw?

Ⓐ $3\frac{1}{4}$ hours
Ⓑ $1\frac{3}{4}$ hours
● $1\frac{7}{8}$ hours
Ⓓ 2 hours

9. Dominic's front yard is a rectangle. It is $15\frac{1}{2}$ feet long and $10\frac{2}{3}$ feet wide. What is the area of Dominic's front yard?

$165\frac{1}{3}$ square feet

10. Samantha ran $2\frac{4}{7}$ miles. Austin ran $2\frac{5}{6}$ times as far. How far did Austin run?

$7\frac{13}{21}$ miles

11. Miss Clark wants to buy fabric to cover her bulletin board. The board is $4\frac{1}{2}$ feet long and 6 feet wide. What is the area that Miss Clark has to cover?

Ⓐ $10\frac{1}{2}$ square feet
Ⓑ $24\frac{1}{2}$ square feet
Ⓒ $27\frac{1}{2}$ square feet
● 27 square feet

12. John is making a model of a pack of gum. The pack is $2\frac{5}{8}$ inches long. He wants to make the model $2\frac{1}{2}$ times as big as the real thing. How long should he make the model?

Ⓐ $4\frac{1}{2}$ inches
Ⓑ $4\frac{1}{3}$ inches
● $6\frac{9}{16}$ inches
Ⓓ $2\frac{1}{2}$ inches

86

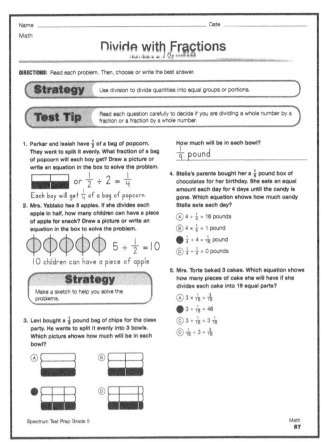

Divide with Fractions
Numbers and Operations

DIRECTIONS: Read each problem. Then, choose or write the best answer.

Strategy Use division to divide quantities into equal groups or portions.

Test Tip Read each question carefully to decide if you are dividing a whole number by a fraction or a fraction by a whole number.

1. Parker and Isaiah have $\frac{1}{2}$ of a bag of popcorn. They want to split it evenly. What fraction of a bag of popcorn will each boy get? Draw a picture or write an equation in the box to solve the problem.

[diagram] or $\frac{1}{2} \div 2 = \frac{1}{4}$

Each boy will get $\frac{1}{4}$ of a bag of popcorn.

2. Mrs. Yablako has 5 apples. If she divides each apple in half, how many children can have a piece of apple for snack? Draw a picture or write an equation in the box to solve the problem.

[diagram] $5 \div \frac{1}{2} = 10$

10 children can have a piece of apple.

Strategy Make a sketch to help you solve the problems.

3. Levi bought a $\frac{1}{3}$ pound bag of chips for the class party. He wants to split it evenly into 3 bowls. Which picture shows how much will be in each bowl?

How much will be in each bowl?

$\frac{1}{9}$ pound

4. Stella's parents bought her a $\frac{1}{4}$ pound box of chocolates for her birthday. She eats an equal amount each day for 4 days until the candy is gone. Which equation shows how much candy Stella eats each day?

Ⓐ $4 \div \frac{1}{4} = 16$ pounds
Ⓑ $4 \times \frac{1}{4} = 1$ pound
● $\frac{1}{4} \div 4 = \frac{1}{16}$ pound
Ⓓ $\frac{1}{4} - \frac{1}{4} = 0$ pounds

5. Mrs. Torte baked 3 cakes. Which equation shows how many pieces of cake she will have if she divides each cake into 16 equal parts?

Ⓐ $3 \times \frac{3}{16} = \frac{3}{16}$
● $3 \div \frac{1}{16} = 48$
Ⓒ $3 + \frac{1}{16} = 3\frac{1}{16}$
Ⓓ $\frac{1}{16} \div 3 = \frac{3}{16}$

87

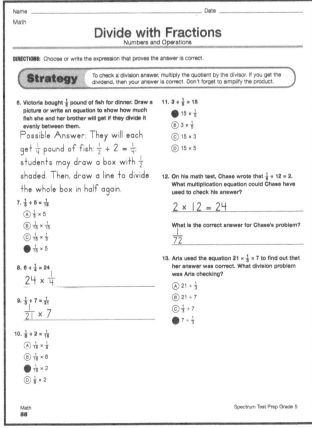

Divide with Fractions
Numbers and Operations

DIRECTIONS: Choose or write the expression that proves the answer is correct.

Strategy To check a division answer, multiply the quotient by the divisor. If you get the dividend, then your answer is correct. Don't forget to simplify the product.

6. Victoria bought $\frac{1}{2}$ pound of fish for dinner. Draw a picture or write an equation to show how much fish she and her brother will get if they divide it evenly between them.

Possible Answer: They will each get $\frac{1}{4}$ pound of fish: $\frac{1}{2} \div 2 = \frac{1}{4}$. Students may draw a box with $\frac{1}{2}$ shaded. Then, draw a line to divide the whole box in half again.

7. $\frac{1}{3} \div 5 = \frac{1}{15}$
Ⓐ $\frac{1}{3} \times 5$
Ⓑ $\frac{1}{15} \times 5$
Ⓒ $\frac{1}{15} \times \frac{1}{3}$
● $\frac{1}{15} \times 5$

8. $6 \div \frac{1}{4} = 24$
$24 \times \frac{1}{4}$

9. $\frac{1}{3} \div 7 = \frac{1}{21}$
$\frac{1}{21} \times 7$

10. $\frac{1}{8} \div 2 = \frac{1}{16}$
Ⓐ $\frac{1}{16} \times \frac{1}{8}$
Ⓑ $\frac{1}{16} \times 8$
Ⓒ $\frac{1}{16} \times 2$
Ⓓ $\frac{1}{8} \div 2$

11. $3 \div \frac{1}{5} = 15$
● $15 \times \frac{1}{5}$
Ⓑ $3 \times \frac{1}{5}$
Ⓒ 15×3
Ⓓ 15×5

12. On his math test, Chase wrote that $\frac{1}{6} \div 12 = 2$. What multiplication equation could Chase have used to check his answer?

$2 \times 12 = 24$

What is the correct answer for Chase's problem?

$\frac{1}{72}$

13. Aria used the equation $21 \times \frac{1}{3} = 7$ to find out her answer was correct. What division problem was Aria checking?

Ⓐ $21 \div \frac{1}{3}$
Ⓑ $21 \div 7$
Ⓒ $\frac{1}{3} \div 7$
● $7 \div \frac{1}{3}$

88

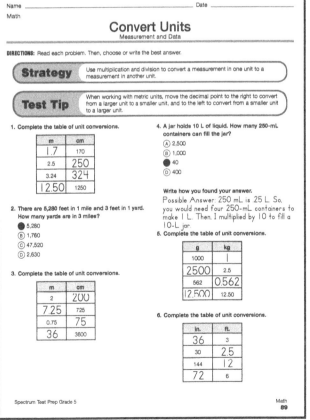

Convert Units
Measurement and Data

DIRECTIONS: Read each problem. Then, choose or write the best answer.

Strategy Use multiplication and division to convert a measurement in one unit to a measurement in another unit.

Test Tip When working with metric units, move the decimal point to the right to convert from a larger unit to a smaller unit, and to the left to convert from a smaller unit to a larger unit.

1. Complete the table of unit conversions.

m	cm
1.7	170
2.5	250
3.24	324
12.50	1250

2. There are 5,280 feet in 1 mile and 3 feet in 1 yard. How many yards are in 3 miles?

● 5,280
Ⓑ 1,760
Ⓒ 47,520
Ⓓ 2,630

3. Complete the table of unit conversions.

m	cm
2	200
7.25	725
0.75	75
36	3600

4. A jar holds 10 L of liquid. How many 250-mL containers can fill the jar?

Ⓐ 2,500
Ⓑ 1,000
● 40
Ⓓ 400

Write how you found your answer.

Possible Answer: 250 mL is .25 L. So, you would need four 250-mL containers to make 1 L. Then, I multiplied by 10 to fill a 10-L jar.

5. Complete the table of unit conversions.

g	kg
1000	1
2500	2.5
562	0.562
12,500	12.50

6. Complete the table of unit conversions.

in.	ft.
36	3
30	2.5
144	12
72	6

89

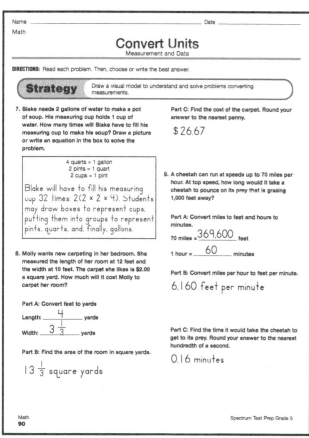

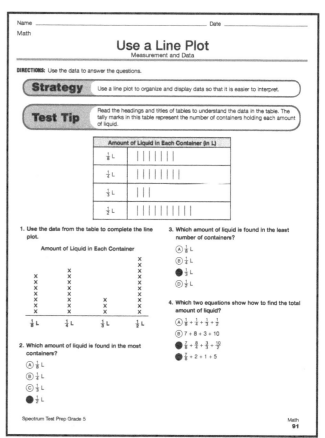

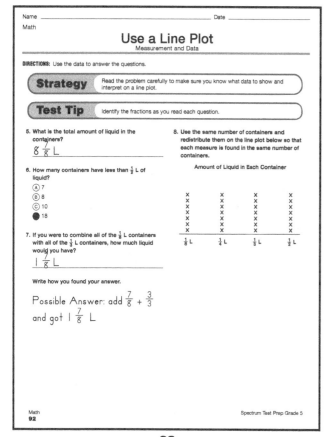

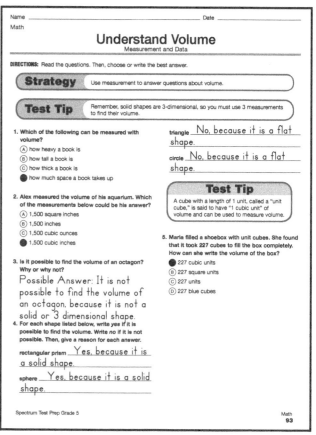

90

91

92

93

Understand Volume
Measurement and Data

Strategy Visualize the situation described in the problem in your head to help you understand what is happening the problem.

6. Aaron used unit cubes to build a rectangular prism. He laid 3 across, 8 back, and stacked them 4 high. What is the volume of his rectangular prism?

96 square units

Write how you know.

Possible Answer: The bottom layer is 3 units wide and 8 units long, so that is an area of 24 units. If you have 4 layers like this, you multiply 24 by 4 to find the total volume.

7. Adam found some bricks in his backyard. Each brick was 1 cubic foot. He stacked them into a cube. There were 5 bricks across, 5 bricks back, and 5 bricks up. How can Adam express the volume of his brick cube?

A) 15 cubic feet
B) 5 cubic feet
C) 50 cubic feet
● 125 cubic feet

8. Malik uses unit cubes to build two figures. He makes a figure that is 5 cubes across, 5 cubes back, and 2 cubes up. He then makes a figure that is 10 cubes across, 2 cubes back, and 2 cubes up. Which figure has the greater volume? Tell how you know.

The first figure has the greater volume because there are 50 cubes in the first shape and 40 cubes in the second shape.

9. Part A: Look at the figure to the right. What is the volume of this prism?

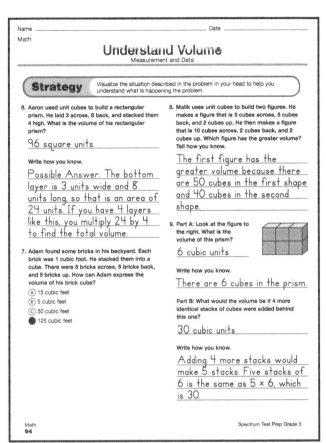

6 cubic units

Write how you know.

There are 6 cubes in the prism.

Part B: What would the volume be if 4 more identical stacks of cubes were added behind this one?

30 cubic units

Write how you know.

Adding 4 more stacks would make 5 stacks. Five stacks of 6 is the same as 5 × 6, which is 30.

94

Find Volume
Measurement and Data

DIRECTIONS: Read each question. Then, choose or write the best answer.

Strategy Use a formula to find volume. When using a formula, think about what each variable means. Substitute the given number for each variable and perform the operation.
Formulas for Volume:
$V = l \times w \times h$
$V = B \times h$ (B is the area of the base)

Test Tip The two formulas above actually mean the same thing. You can replace $l \times w$ with B, because the area of the base is found by multiplying the length by the width.

1. Tristan measured his bookshelf. He found that it is 1 foot wide, 3 feet long, and 6 feet tall. What is the volume of Tristan's bookshelf?

A) 18 feet
B) 10 square feet
● 18 cubic feet
D) 10 cubic feet

Write how you found your answer.

I multiplied 1 × 3 × 6.

2. Mrs. Weinstein has a stack of math books on her desk. One math book has an area of 99 square inches. The stack is 12 inches high. How much space is the stack of math books taking up?

1,188 cubic inches

3. Sydney wants to send a birthday gift to her cousin. She has a box that is 6 inches wide, 6 inches long, and 4 inches deep. Is the box large enough for a gift with a volume of 125 cubic inches?

yes

Write how you know.

6 × 6 × 4 = 144 cubic inches. The box is larger than the present.

4. Which boxes have a volume larger than this box?

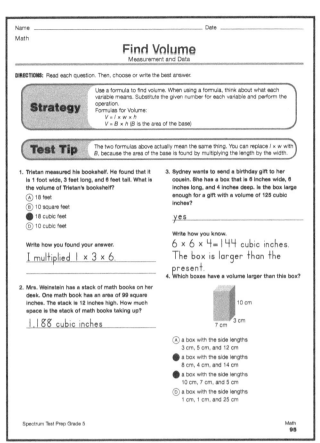

A) a box with the side lengths 3 cm, 5 cm, and 12 cm
● a box with the side lengths 8 cm, 4 cm, and 14 cm
● a box with the side lengths 10 cm, 7 cm, and 5 cm
D) a box with the side lengths 1 cm, 1 cm, and 25 cm

95

Find Volume
Measurement and Data

Strategy Draw shapes described in word problems and label measurements given. Use the drawing to solve the problem.

Test Tip If you use more than one prism to create a shape, you can add their individual volumes to find the volume of the whole shape.

5. Julian got an autographed basketball from his favorite team. He wants to put it in a protective box. The basketball has a volume of 456 cubic inches. He went to the store and found 3 protective cases for sports balls.

Box A is a cube with a side length of 5 inches
Box B is a cube with a side length of 8 inches
Box C is a cube with a side length of 10 inches

Which box should Julian buy for his ball? Why?

Possible Answer: He should buy Box B. The volume is 512 cubic inches. Box A would be too small, and Box C would be too big.

6. Mr. and Mrs. Hale have a pool in their backyard. To know what chemicals to put in it, they need to know how much water it holds. The pool is 4 feet deep, 8 feet wide, and 12 feet long. What is the volume of the pool?

A) 96 cubic feet
B) 32 cubic feet
C) 48 cubic feet
● 384 cubic feet

7. One cubic foot of water is equal to about $7\frac{1}{2}$ gallons. One part of the public pool is 6 feet deep, 25 feet long, and 18 feet wide. How many gallons of water can it hold?

20,250 gallons

8. Bella found some old boxes around the house and decided to make something out of them. The picture below shows what she made. If the two boxes on top are congruent and the bottom box is a cube, what is the volume of the entire figure?

6,552 cubic inches

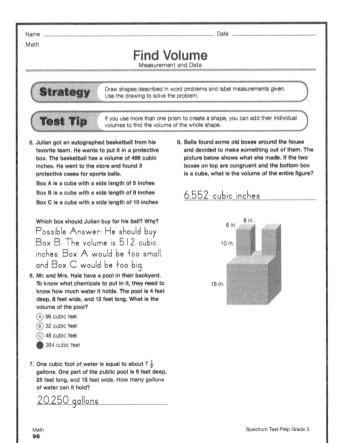

6 in. 6 in.
10 in.
18 in.

96

Graph Points
Geometry

DIRECTIONS: Use the coordinate grid to answer the questions.

Strategy Graph data by plotting points on the coordinate grid. Each point is identified by an ordered pair written in the form (x, y). So, the first number in the pair corresponds to a point on the x (horizontal) axis, and the second number corresponds to a point on the y (vertical) axis.

Test Tip When identifying points on a coordinate grid, always start at the origin (0, 0). Move along the x-axis, and then, along the y-axis. Count the lines on the grid, not the spaces.

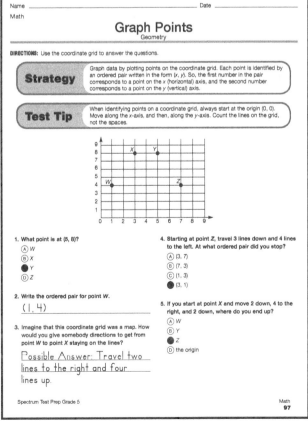

1. What point is at (5, 8)?
A) W
B) X
● Y
D) Z

2. Write the ordered pair for point W.
(1, 4)

3. Imagine that this coordinate grid was a map. How would you give somebody directions to get from point W to point X staying on the lines?

Possible Answer: Travel two lines to the right and four lines up.

4. Starting at point Z, travel 3 lines down and 4 lines to the left. At what ordered pair did you stop?
A) (3, 7)
B) (7, 3)
C) (1, 3)
● (3, 1)

5. If you start at point X and move 2 down, 4 to the right, and 2 down, where do you end up?
A) W
B) Y
● Z
D) the origin

97

Graph Points
Geometry

Strategy Always plot points on the grid the same way you identify them. Start at the origin, move along the *x*-axis. Then, move along the *y*-axis.

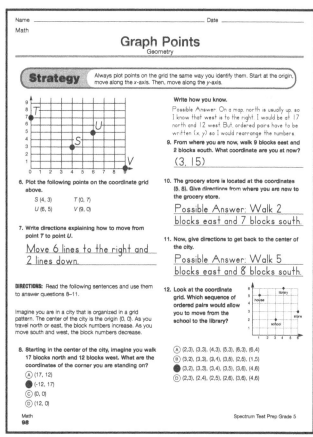

Write how you know.
Possible Answer: On a map, north is usually up, so I know that west is to the right. I would be at 17 north and 12 west. But, ordered pairs have to be written (x, y) so I would rearrange the numbers.

9. From where you are now, walk 9 blocks east and 2 blocks south. What coordinate are you at now?
(3, 15)

6. Plot the following points on the coordinate grid above.
S (4, 3)   T (0, 7)
U (6, 5)   V (9, 0)

10. The grocery store is located at the coordinates (5, 8). Give directions from where you are now to the grocery store.
Possible Answer: Walk 2 blocks east and 7 blocks south.

7. Write directions explaining how to move from point *T* to point *U*.
Move 6 lines to the right and 2 lines down.

11. Now, give directions to get back to the center of the city.
Possible Answer: Walk 5 blocks east and 8 blocks south.

DIRECTIONS: Read the following sentences and use them to answer questions 8–11.

Imagine you are in a city that is organized in a grid pattern. The center of the city is the origin (0, 0). As you travel north or east, the block numbers increase. As you move south and west, the block numbers decrease.

8. Starting in the center of the city, imagine you walk 17 blocks north and 12 blocks west. What are the coordinates of the corner you are standing on?
(A) (17, 12)
● (-12, 17)
(C) (0, 0)
(D) (12, 0)

12. Look at the coordinate grid. Which sequence of ordered pairs would allow you to move from the school to the library?

(A) (2,3), (3,3), (4,3), (5,3), (6,3), (6,4)
● (3,2), (3,3), (3,4), (3,5), (2,5), (1,5)
(C) (3,2), (3,3), (3,4), (3,5), (3,6), (4,6)
(D) (2,3), (2,4), (2,5), (2,6), (3,6), (4,6)

98

Classify 2-D Shapes
Geometry

DIRECTIONS: Name and draw the described polygon.

Strategy Use the characteristics of polygons to classify them.

Test Tip Remember that two-dimensional shapes are categorized by their characteristics, such as number of sides and angles and whether they have parallel and perpendicular lines.

1. Polygon with three equal sides
Shape: equilateral triangle
[student should draw an equilateral triangle]

2. Polygon with opposite sides equal and four right angles
Shape: rectangle
[student should draw a rectangle]

3. Polygon with three sides of different lengths
Shape: scalene triangle
[student should draw a scalene triangle]

4. Polygon with four sides equal, opposite sides parallel, and four angles equal
Shape: square
[student should draw a square]

5. Which of the following shapes is NOT a quadrilateral?
(A) parallelogram
● pentagon
(C) rhombus
(D) square

Write how you know.
Quadrilaterals are shapes that have 4 sides. A pentagon has 5 sides.

99

Classify 2-D Shapes
Geometry

DIRECTIONS: Read each question. Then, choose or write the best answer.

Strategy Read each description carefully and use the characteristics described in the problem and the characteristics of shapes to sketch the shape. Use the sketch to solve the problem.

6. I am a quadrilateral.
I am a parallelogram.
I have 4 right angles.
My opposite sides are congruent.
Who am I?
rectangle

7. I am a quadrilateral.
I am a parallelogram.
I have no right angles.
All of my sides are congruent.
Who am I?
rhombus

8. I am a 3-sided polygon.
I have no congruent sides.
I have a right angle.
Who am I?
right, scalene triangle

9. Place the names of the shapes in the graphic organizer from the most general name at the top to the most specific name at the bottom.

[rectangle
parallelogram
square
polygon
quadrilateral]

polygon
quadrilateral
parallelogram
rectangle
square

10. Which of these terms describes a rhombus? Choose three.
● polygon
(B) square
● parallelogram
● quadrilateral

100

Strategy Review

Strategy Apply prior knowledge and basic operations to solve problems.

You can use what you know about number relationships and computation skills to solve real-world problems.

EXAMPLE
Miss Lacy bought 6 pounds of apples at $1.99 per pound, 2 cartons of eggs at $2.69 per dozen, and 5 cans of cat food at $1.39 each. She had a coupon for $0.50 off each can of cat food. How much was Miss Lacy's total bill before tax?

First, write an expression to model the problem.
(6 × 1.99) + (2 × 2.69) + 5 (1.39 − .50)

Next, use order of operations to evaluate the expression.

Evaluate parentheses first: (11.94) + (5.38) + 5 (0.89) =
Multiply from left to right: (11.94) + (5.38) + 4.45 =
Add from left to right: 11.94 + 5.38 + 4.45 = $21.77

Mis Lacy's bill was $21.77.

1. Miles has $475. He spends $125 on new school clothes. Then, three of his relatives each give him $25 for his birthday. Finally, Miles divides the remaining money into three equal amounts. He puts one part into his college fund and one part into his savings account. He keeps the third part. Write and evaluate an expression to show how much money Miles has.

$\frac{(475 - 125)}{3} + (3 \times 25)$:

$ 141.67

2. On Thursday, Alexandra's teacher assigned her to read a book by the following Tuesday. The book has 450 pages. She thinks she can read 75 pages on weekdays and 150 pages each on Saturday and Sunday. Does Alexandra have enough time to finish the book if she starts reading on Thursday? Write and evaluate an expression to find the answer.

450 − (3 × 75) − (2 × 150);
Yes, she will have enough time.

How did the strategy help you answer these questions?
Possible answer: I wrote an expression and then, I used order of operations to evaluate it.

101

Answer Key
126

Spectrum Test Prep Grade 5

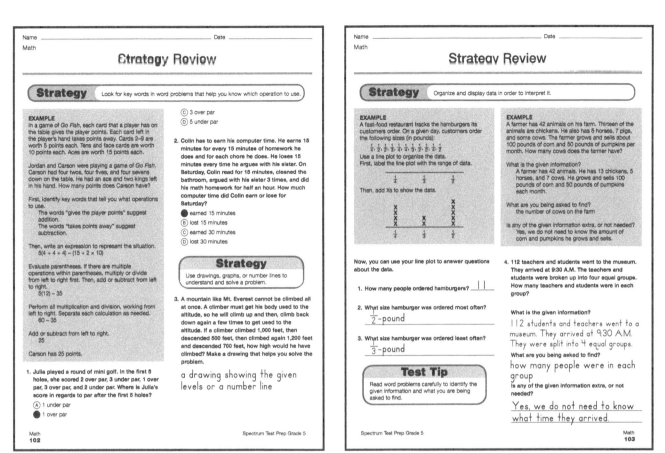

Strategy Review

Strategy — Look for key words in word problems that help you know which operation to use.

EXAMPLE
In a game of *Go Fish*, each card that a player has on the table gives the player points. Each card left in the player's hand takes points away. Cards 2–9 are worth 5 points each. Tens and face cards are worth 10 points each. Aces are worth 15 points each.

Jordan and Carson were playing a game of *Go Fish*. Carson had four twos, four fives, and four sevens down on the table. He had an ace and two kings left in his hand. How many points does Carson have?

First, identify key words that tell you what operations to use.
The words "gives the player points" suggest addition.
The words "takes points away" suggest subtraction.

Then, write an expression to represent the situation.
$5(4 + 4 + 4) - (15 + 2 \times 10)$

Evaluate parentheses. If there are multiple operations within parentheses, multiply or divide from left to right first. Then, add or subtract from left to right.
$5(12) - 35$

Perform all multiplication and division, working from left to right. Separate each calculation as needed.
$60 - 35$

Add or subtract from left to right.
25

Carson has 25 points.

1. Julia played a round of mini golf. In the first 5 holes, she scored 2 over par, 3 under par, 1 over par, 3 over par, and 2 under par. Where is Julia's score in regards to par after the first 5 holes?
Ⓐ 1 under par
● 1 over par

Ⓒ 3 over par
Ⓓ 5 under par

2. Colin has to earn his computer time. He earns 15 minutes for every 15 minutes of homework he does and for each chore he does. He loses 15 minutes every time he argues with his sister. On Saturday, Colin read for 15 minutes, cleaned the bathroom, argued with his sister 3 times, and did his math homework for half an hour. How much computer time did Colin earn or lose for Saturday?
● earned 15 minutes
Ⓑ lost 15 minutes
Ⓒ earned 30 minutes
Ⓓ lost 30 minutes

Strategy — Use drawings, graphs, or number lines to understand and solve a problem.

3. A mountain like Mt. Everest cannot be climbed all at once. A climber must get his body used to the altitude, so he will climb up and then, climb back down again a few times to get used to the altitude. If a climber climbed 1,000 feet, then descended 500 feet, then climbed again 1,200 feet and descended 700 feet, how high would he have climbed? Make a drawing that helps you solve the problem.

a drawing showing the given levels or a number line

102

Strategy Review

Strategy — Organize and display data in order to interpret it.

EXAMPLE
A fast-food restaurant tracks the hamburgers its customers order. On a given day, customers order the following sizes (in pounds):
$\frac{1}{2}, \frac{1}{2}, \frac{1}{3}, \frac{1}{4}, \frac{1}{2}, \frac{1}{3}, \frac{1}{2}, \frac{1}{2}, \frac{1}{3}, \frac{1}{2}, \frac{1}{2}$
Use a line plot to organize the data.
First, label the line plot with the range of data.

Then, add Xs to show the data.

```
X                    X
X                    X
X          X         X
X          X         X
X          X         X
----------------------
1/4        1/3       1/2
```

Now, you can use your line plot to answer questions about the data.

1. How many people ordered hamburgers? ___11___

2. What size hamburger was ordered most often?
$\frac{1}{2}$-pound

3. What size hamburger was ordered least often?
$\frac{1}{3}$-pound

Test Tip
Read word problems carefully to identify the given information and what you are being asked to find.

EXAMPLE
A farmer has 42 animals on his farm. Thirteen of the animals are chickens. He also has 5 horses, 7 pigs, and some cows. The farmer grows and sells about 100 pounds of corn and 50 pounds of pumpkins per month. How many cows does the farmer have?

What is the given information?
A farmer has 42 animals. He has 13 chickens, 5 horses, and 7 cows. He grows and sells 100 pounds of corn and 50 pounds of pumpkins each month.

What are you being asked to find?
the number of cows on the farm

Is any of the given information extra, or not needed?
Yes, we do not need to know the amount of corn and pumpkins he grows and sells.

4. 112 teachers and students went to the museum. They arrived at 9:30 A.M. The teachers and students were broken up into four equal groups. How many teachers and students were in each group?

What is the given information?
112 students and teachers went to a museum. They arrived at 9:30 A.M. They were split into 4 equal groups.

What are you being asked to find?
how many people were in each group

Is any of the given information extra, or not needed?
Yes, we do not need to know what time they arrived.

103

Strategy Review

Strategy — Use rules, properties, or formulas to solve problems.

EXAMPLE
Ruby received a package in the mail that came in a 12 in. by 13 in. by 7 in. box. Use the formula for volume, $V = l \times w \times h$ or $V = Bh$, to find the volume of the carton.

```
       7 in.
   12 in.  13 in.
```

First, write the formula for the volume of a right rectangular prism.
$V = l \times w \times h$

Put the measurements into the formula.
$V = l \times w \times h = 12 \times 13 \times 7 = 1,092$

The volume of the box is 1,092 in.³

1. Ruby has a chest in her room that is 18 inches tall, 4 feet long, and 2 feet wide. What is the volume of the chest?

20,736 in.³ or 12 ft³

2. Hudson is painting his wall. The wall is 10 feet long and 8 feet high. What is the area that Hudson will be painting?
Ⓐ 16 ft²
● 80 ft²
Ⓒ 180 ft²
Ⓓ 38 ft²

3. Hudson wants to put a border all around his room. If all of Hudson's walls are the same dimensions, how long must the border be to fit all the way around the room?
Ⓐ 10 feet
Ⓑ 25 feet
● 40 feet
Ⓓ 50 feet

104